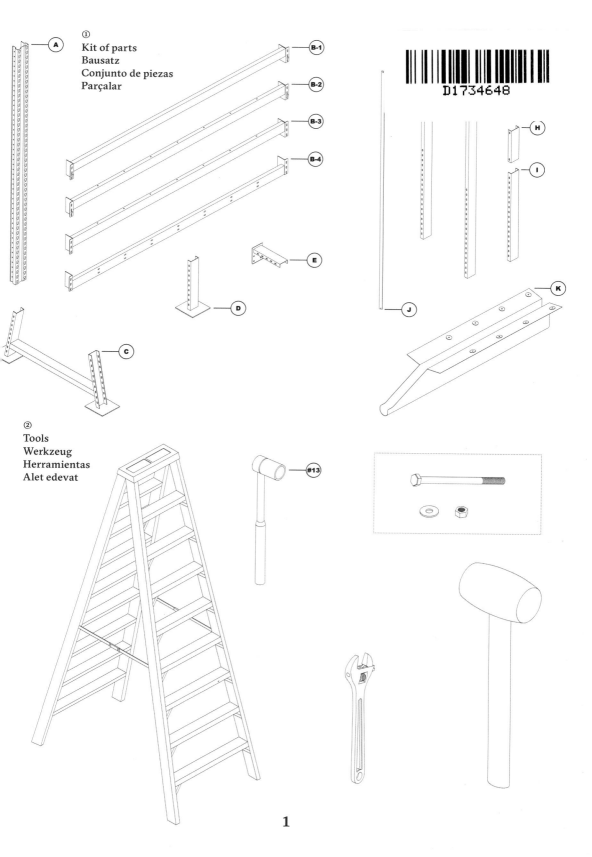

① Kit of parts
Bausatz
Conjunto de piezas
Parçalar

D1734648

② Tools
Werkzeug
Herramientas
Alet edevat

#13

1

Core
Basis
Pieza Principal
Kaide

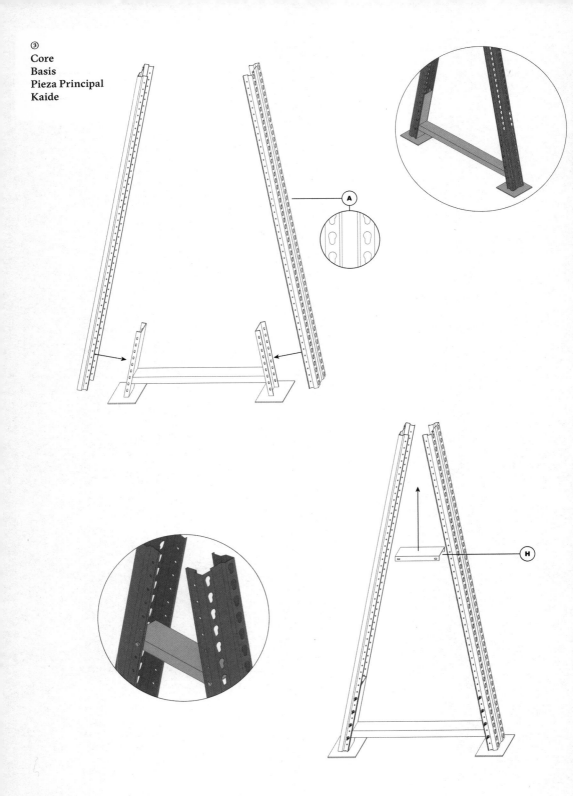

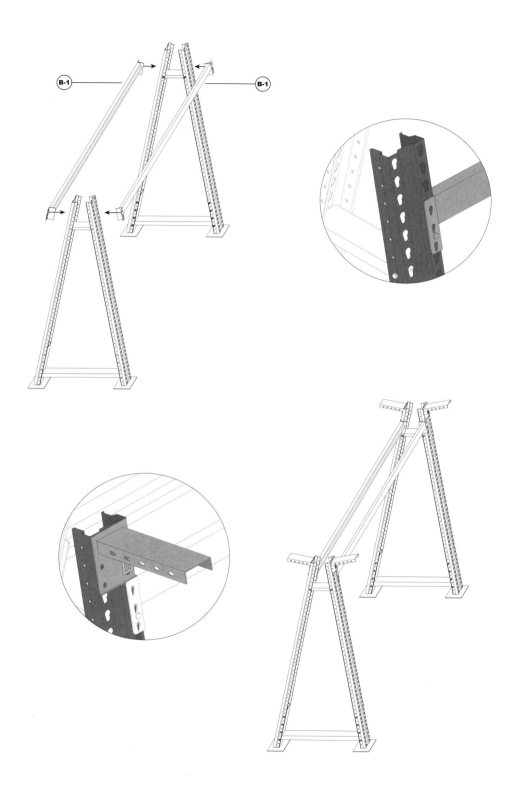

④
Roof system A
Dachsystem A
Sistema de techo A
Çatı sistemi A

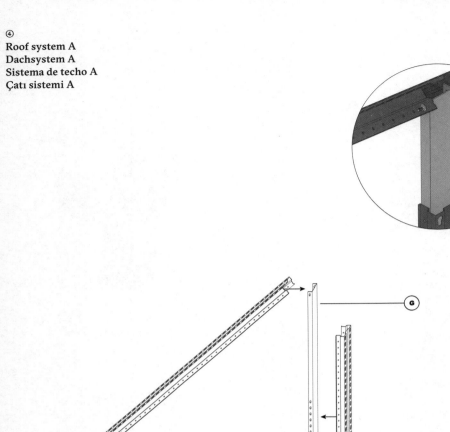

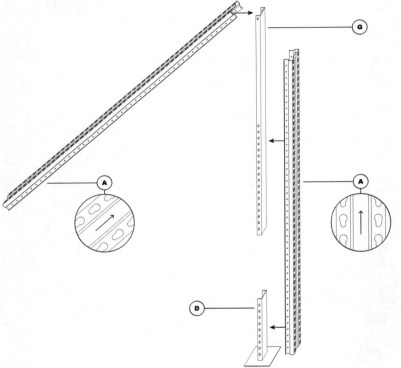

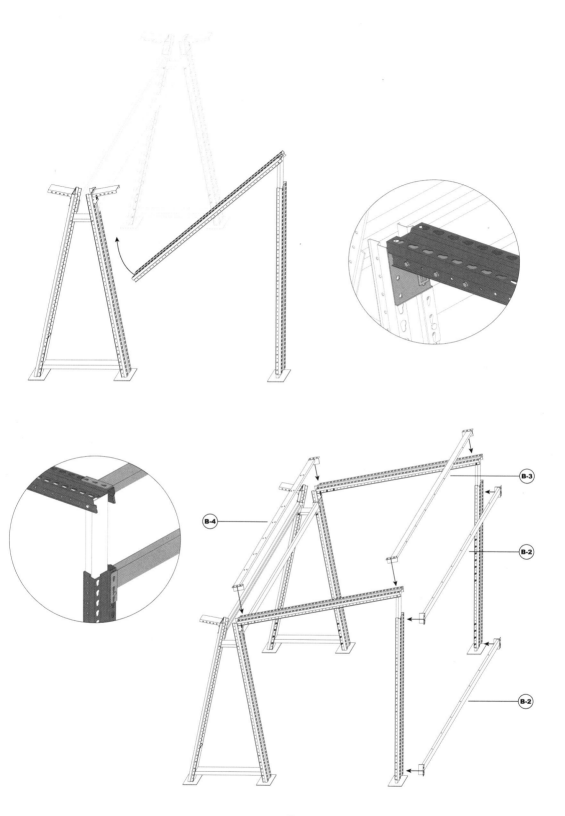

B-3

B-4

B-2

B-2

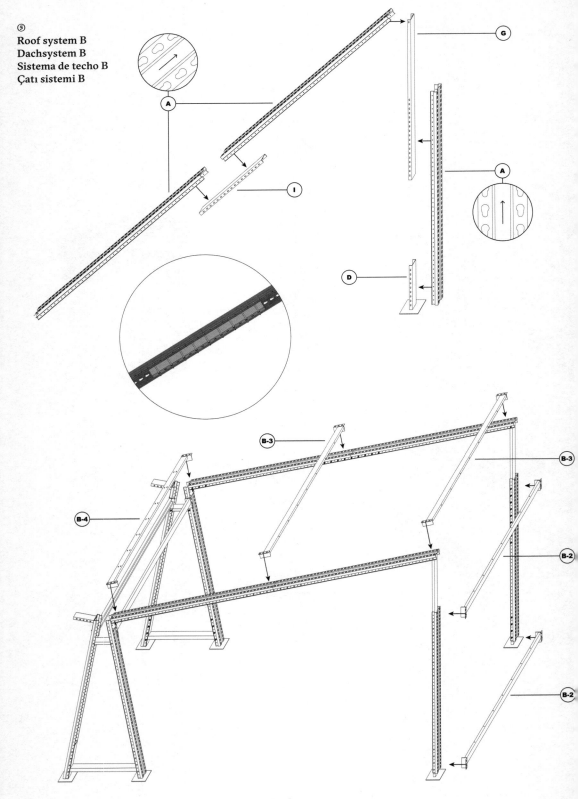

⑤
Roof system B
Dachsystem B
Sistema de techo B
Çatı sistemi B

6

⑥
Roof system C
Dachsystem C
Sistema de techo C
Çatı sistemi C

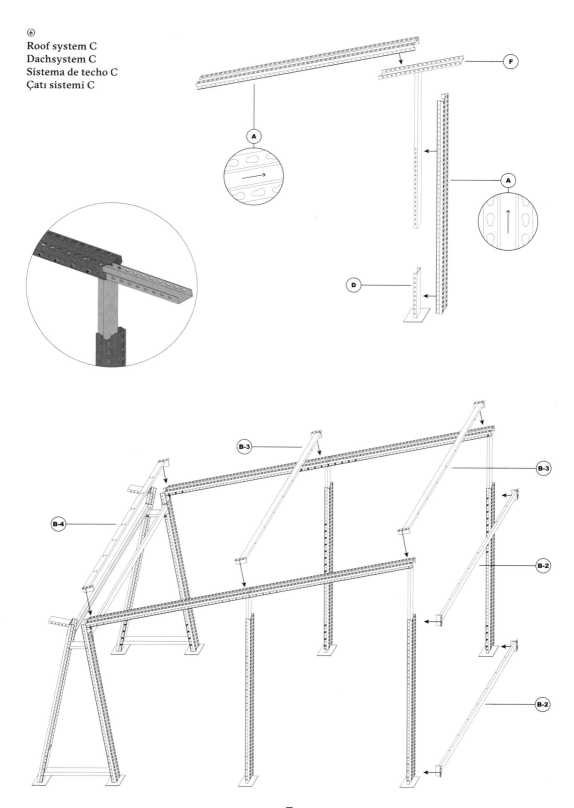

⑦
X-brace
X-Strebe
Tirante
Payandalar

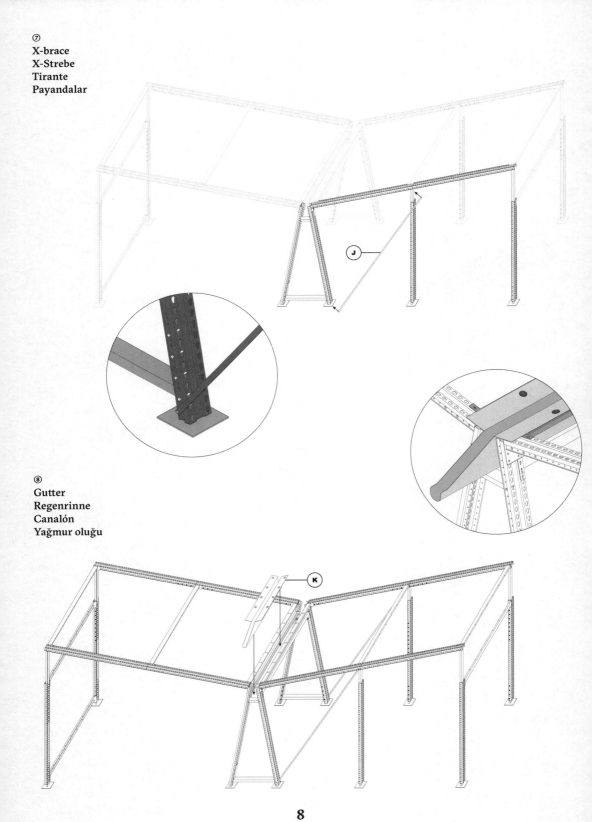

⑧
Gutter
Regenrinne
Canalón
Yağmur oluğu

8

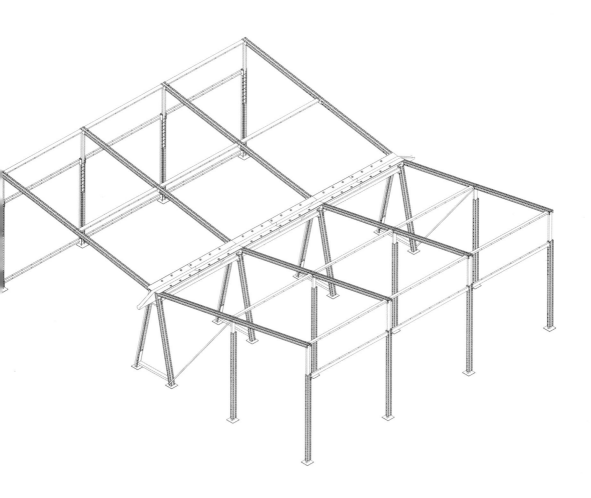

Estudio Teddy Cruz + Forman: The Retrofit Gecekondu

Estudio Teddy Cruz + Forman: Das Retrofit-Gecekondu

en

Kotti & Co engage with the sociopolitical dimensions of housing, demanding transformations in housing policy and finance. From the tenants' encounter around the urgency of affordability, a neighborhood platform was formed for knowledge exchange and bottom-up planning. As this dialogue unfolded, a physical space emerged in the form of the Gecekondu. Built as an informal retrofit to an undifferentiated public space in Berlin-Kreuzberg, it has exposed the socioeconomic and political dynamics often missing from the housing question. Kotti & Co's Gecekondu physicalizes a notion that has been fundamental to our work at the Tijuana–San Diego border: the re-threading of public space and housing, demonstrating that housing is not only about dwelling units but is also a process that can carve new spaces of socialization within the mono-culture and mono-economy that neoliberalism is installing in the contemporary city.

The circulation of knowledge between Kotti & Co and Estudio Teddy Cruz + Forman has resulted in a design organized around the relation between informal urbanization and housing. It is based on the social and material strategies of retrofit and adaption. Our proposal aims to elevate the capacity of the Gecekondu into a distributive system, able to support a variety of socioeconomic, political, and cultural activities in the context of housing.

We propose a light infrastructural system that can be easily transported and assembled. This system consists of the recombination of existing "off-the-shelf" industrial storage elements to generate a series of newly designed armatures, which will be open to adaptation using locally available materials. We envisage an architecture of parts that can anticipate spatial configurations according to local need, ranging from self-help housing additions to an assembly hall for a temporary urban parliament.

What are required today to advance the housing question is not just new designs but also infiltration into the exclusionary politics and economics of housing.

de

Mit ihrem Einsatz für Veränderungen in der Wohnungspolitik und -wirtschaft setzen Kotti & Co ihren Schwerpunkt auf die politische Dimension der Wohnungsfrage. Aus dem Zusammenschluss der Mieter um die akute Frage nach bezahlbarem Wohnraum hat sich eine Nachbarschaftsplattform für Wissensaustausch und Stadtplanung von unten formiert. Gleichzeitig mit dem Dialog entstand ein konkreter Raum in Form des Gecekondu. Was als informelles „Retrofit" in einem undifferenzierten öffentlichen Raum in Berlin-Kreuzberg begann, hat die sozialen, ökonomischen und politischen Faktoren offengelegt, die in der Wohnungsfrage häufig nicht berücksichtigt werden. Wir verstehen das Gecekondu von Kotti & Co als die Manifestation einer Idee, die für unsere Arbeit an der Grenze Tijuana-San Diego von grundlegender Bedeutung ist: die neuerliche Verbindung von öffentlichem Raum und Wohnen, die zeigt, dass es beim Wohnungsbau nicht nur um Wohneinheiten geht, sondern auch um einen Prozess, der innerhalb der neoliberalen Monokultur und -ökonomie unserer Städte neue soziale Räume erschließen kann.

Das Ergebnis des gegenseitigen Lernprozesses zwischen Kotti & Co und Estudio Teddy Cruz + Forman ist ein Entwurf, in dessen Zentrum die Beziehung zwischen informeller Urbanisierung und Wohnen steht. Er beruht auf den sozialen und materiellen Strategien von Nachrüstung, Anpassung und Aneignung. Mit unserem Vorschlag wollen wir die Funktionen des Gecekondu in ein distribuierbares System übertragen, das die Möglichkeit bietet, verschiedene sozioökonomische, politische und kulturelle Aktivitäten im Zusammenhang mit dem Wohnen zu unterstützen.

Unser Entwurf besteht aus einem leichten Infrastruktursystem, das sich einfach transportieren und aufbauen lässt. In diesem System werden Standardelemente für industrielle Lagersysteme neu kombiniert und zu einem flexiblen Gerüst zusammengestellt, das mithilfe lokal verfügbarer Materialien erweitert werden kann. Uns schwebt eine Architektur

Estudio Teddy Cruz + Forman: El Gecekondu adaptado

Estudio Teddy Cruz + Forman: Tadil / Retrofit Gecekondu

es

Kotti & Co se implica con los aspectos sociopolíticos de la vivienda, exigiendo transformaciones en las políticas de financiación del alquiler. A partir del encuentro de los inquilinos en torno a la urgente demanda de precios accesibles, se constituyó una plataforma de barrio para el intercambio de conocimientos y una planificación de base social. Al ir desarrollándose este diálogo, fue emergiendo un espacio físico dando forma al Gecekondu. Construida como un acto de adaptación informal de un espacio público en Berlín-Kreuzberg, esta estructura física ha manifestado las dinámicas socioeconómicas y políticas que a menudo están ausentes en la cuestión de la vivienda. El Gecekondu de Kotti & Co es la materialización de un concepto que ha sido fundamental en nuestra práctica urbanística y arquitectónica en la frontera Tijuana-San Diego: el entramado del espacio público con la vivienda, que demuestra que la cuestión de la vivienda no consiste solamente en la vivienda en si misma, sino en un proceso complejo que puede abrir nuevos espacios y programas de socialización dentro de la monocultura y la monoeconomía que el neoliberalismo está instalando en la ciudad contemporánea.

La circulación de conocimientos entre Kotti & Co y Estudio Teddy Cruz + Forman ha dado lugar a un diseño organizado en torno a la relación entre urbanización informal y vivienda. Se basa en las estrategias materiales y sociales de alteración y adaptación. Nuestra propuesta apunta a elevar la capacidad del Gecekondu para hacer de él un sistema difundible, capaz de dar soporte a una variedad de actividades socioeconómicas, políticas y culturales en el contexto de la vivienda.

Proponemos un sistema de infraestructura ligera que puede ser transportado y montado fácilmente. Este sistema emerge de la recombinación de elementos existentes de almacenamiento industrial prefabricados, para diseñar una serie de armazones nuevos que puedan abrirse a la adaptación utilizando materiales disponibles localmente. Podemos imaginar una arquitectura de piezas que pueden anticipar diversas configuraciones espaciales en función de las necesidades

tr

Kotti & Co konut sorunun sosyopolitik boyutuyla ilgilenir, konutlandırma ve konutların finansmanı politikalarında değişimler talep eder. Konut giderlerinin karşılanabilir olmasının önceliği konusuna yoğunlaşmış kiracı toplantılarından bilgi alışverişi ve tabandan yukarı bir planlamayı hedefleyen bir komşuluk platformu doğmuştu. Diyalog geliştikçe Gecekondu projesiyle fiziki bir mekân ortaya çıktı. Berlin-Kreuzberg'deki işlevlendirilmemiş bir kamusal alana informel bir retrofit olarak inşa edilen Gecekondu konutlandırma sorununda sıkça ıskalanan sosyoekonomik ve siyasi dinamiklere ışık tutu. Kotti&Co'nun Gecekondu'su Tijuana–San Diego sınırındaki çalışmalarımızda asli önemi olan bir kavramı somutlaştırdı: Kamusal mekânların ve konutların tekrar ilişkilendirilmesi ve bu yapılırken konut sorunun sadece bir barınma birimi sorunu değil aynı zamanda neoliberalizmin çağdaş şehrin bir parçası haline getirdiği mono-kültür ve mono-ekonomi içersinde yeni sosyalizasyon alanları için gedikler açabilecek bir süreçle ilgili olduğunun da gösterilmesi.

Kotti & Co ve Estudio Teddy Cruz + Forman arasında bilgi akışının sağlanması informel şehirleşme ve konutlandırma arasındaki ilişkinin etrafında yeni bir tasarımın gelişmesiyle sonuçlandı. Bu tasarım tadil/ retrofit ve uyarlamanın sosyal ve maddi stratejileri üzerine bina edilmiştir. Hedefimiz Gecekondu'nun sunduklarını, konut sorunu bağlamında farklı sosyoekonomik, siyasi ve kültürel faaliyetleri destekleyen, paylaşılabilir bir sistem düzeyine yükseltmek.

Kolayca taşınabilen ve kurulabilen, hafif bir altyapı sistemi öneriyoruz. Bu sistem piyasada mevcut, sıradan endüstriyel depolama sistemi malzemelerinin, yepyeni bir tasarım ürünü ve yerel olarak ulaşılabilir malzemenin uyarlanmasına açık bir dizi yapı öğesinin üretilmesi amacıyla farklı bir şekilde kullanılmasını içeriyor. Yerel ihtiyaçlara göre, insanların evlerine kendi başlarına ekleyebilecekleri mekânlardan geçici şehir meclisi için toplantı salonuna kadar farklı mekânsal çözümler öngörebilen bir öğeler mimarisi tahayyül ediyoruz.

Affordability must be connected to the politics of labor, regarding job generation and entrepreneurship in Berlin, but also in Tijuana and elsewhere. Amplification of the potential of the layered construction systems of informal urbanization is necessary in order to re-think affordability in slum housing. We propose that the prefabricated parts of our distributive Gecekondu are manufactured by one of the multinational factories (*maquiladoras*) in Tijuana, pointing towards the importance of investing in the slums from which they solicit their required labor-force. Scaled up, the serial production of these housing parts would allow easy distribution by municipalities and local activist groups, enabling material and economic top-down support for bottom-up processes.

der Bauteile vor, die räumliche Konfigurationen an lokale Bedürfnisse anpassen kann – vom selbstorganisierten Hausanbau bis zum Versammlungsort für ein temporäres Stadtparlament.

Um die Wohnungsfrage voranzubringen, reichen Gestaltungsentwürfe jedoch nicht aus; ebenso wichtig ist es, die Ausgrenzungsmechanismen der Wohnungspolitik und -ökonomie zu unterlaufen. Das Problem bezahlbaren Wohnraums muss mit der Arbeitspolitik verknüpft werden, indem nicht nur in Berlin, sondern auch in Tijuana und anderswo Arbeitsplätze geschaffen und Kleinbetriebe unterstützt werden. Um dieses Problem in den Slums neu zu denken, muss das Potenzial der vielschichtigen Konstruktionsprinzipien informeller Urbanisierung aufgegriffen und weiterentwickelt werden. Wir schlagen vor, die Fertigteile unseres zur Distribution bestimmten Gecekondu von einer der multinationalen Fabriken (*maquiladoras*) in Tijuana herstellen zu lassen. So lässt sich Notwendigkeit von Investitionen in den Slums , aus denen diese Firma ihre Arbeitskräfte bezieht, klar aufzeigen. In größerem Maßstab würde die Serienfertigung dieser Bauteile eine einfache Verteilung durch Gemeinden und lokale Aktionsgruppen und damit eine materielle und wirtschaftliche Unterstützung von oben für urbane Prozesse von unten ermöglichen.

locales, desde posibles extensiones pasando por viviendas autoconstruidas, hasta un salón público que actúe como parlamento urbano temporal.

Lo que se requiere hoy para avanzar en el problema de la vivienda no sólo involucra nuevos diseños, sino también la infiltración en las políticas y las economías de vivienda excluyentes. La asequibilidad debe estar vinculada con las políticas laborales, en lo relativo a la generación de empleos y al desarrollo del espíritu empresarial en Berlín, pero también en Tijuana y en otros lugares. Es necesario incrementar el potencial de la construcción en capas, que caracteriza a la urbanización informal, a fin de repensar la asequibilidad de la vivienda en los asentamientos informales. Proponemos que las piezas prefabricadas de nuestro Gecekondu difundible emerjan de una de las fábricas trasnacionales (*maquiladoras*) en Tijuana, apuntando a la necesidad de inversión en los barrios marginales desde donde se extrae la fuerza laboral de fabricación. La producción en serie de estas piezas para la construcción de vivienda, llevada a mayor escala, permitiría una fácil distribución por parte de los municipios y los grupos de activistas locales, vinculando así los sistemas materiales y económicos que vienen de arriba hacia abajo, con los procesos urbanos emergentes de abajo hacia arriba.

Konut sorunu çözmek için bugün gereken sadece yeni tasarımlar değil aynı zamanda resmi konutlandırmanın dışlayıcı ekonomisi ve siyasetine sızmaktır da. Mali olarak karşılanabilirlik, emek politikalarıyla muhakkak surette ilişiklendirilmelidir, özellikle de yeni iş alanlarının yaratılması ve girişimciliğin desteklenmesi babında ve sadece Berlin'de değil Tijuana ve başka yerlerde de. Varoşlardaki konut soruna mali açıdan karşılanabilir yeni bir çözüm bulabilmek için informel şehirleşmenin katmanlı yapı sistemlerinin potansiyelinin geliştirilmesi gerekir. Bizim paylaşımcı Gecekondu'muzun prefabrik yapı elemanlarının Tijuana'daki çokuluslu şirket fabrikalarından birinde (*maquiladoras*) üretilmesini öneriyoruz, böylelikle bu şirketlerin ihtiyaçları olan ucuz iş gücünü talep ettikleri varoşlara yatırım yapmalarının önemini vurgulamış olacağız. Daha geniş bakıldığında, yapı elemanlarının seri halde üretimi, belediyeler ve yerel aktivist gruplar tarafından daha kolay dağıtılmalarına da olanak sağlayacak, bu da aşağıdan yukarı süreçlerin, mali ve aynı olarak yukarıdan aşağıya desteklenebilmesini mümkün kılacaktır.

Production   Produktion

Mecalux factory, Tijuana
Mecalux-Fabrik, Tijuana
Fábrica Mecalux, Tijuana
Mecalux fabrikası, Tijuana

Producción   Üretim

Test set-up
Probeaufbau
Prueba de construcción
Test kurulumu

Test set-up
Probeaufbau
Prueba de construcción
Test kurulumu

17

A Conversation between San Diego, Tijuana, and Berlin

Ein Gespräch zwischen San Diego, Tijuana und Berlin

en

With Teddy Cruz and Fonna Forman (Estudio Teddy Cruz + Forman), Ulrike Hamann, Melanie Dyck, Zehra Ulutürk, Alexander Sandy Kaltenborn, Fatma Cakmak, and Angelika Levi (Kotti & Co), and Jesko Fezer (*Wohnungsfrage*)

de

Mit Teddy Cruz und Fonna Forman (Estudio Teddy Cruz + Forman), Ulrike Hamann, Melanie Dyck, Zehra Ulutürk, Alexander Sandy Kaltenborn, Fatma Cakmak und Angelika Levi (Kotti & Co) sowie Jesko Fezer (*Wohnungsfrage*)

Ulrike   Our situation is not bad because of bad architecture. We have comfortable flats, which we want to keep as our homes. But there is the economic dimension to housing, which is how to pay the rent in the increasingly neoliberal housing market. Housing is never only about the houses themselves.

Melanie   Many issues around housing are invisible from the outside, for example, when up to ten people live in a single-family apartment. This is invisible from the street. It remains within the apartments, as do the high utility bills. They apply to everyone, but they affect people differently according to their conditions. These divisions determine what social housing really means.

Zehra   When we started our protest movement at Kotti, I thought this problem only existed in Kreuzberg. I soon realized that it affects the whole city—and after a few nationwide demonstrations it became clear to me that the problem can be found everywhere in this country. And since we have met you, Teddy and Fonna, it is obvious that it affects the entire world. The politicians try to cover up the problem of housing; it is therefore up to us to make it visible.

Teddy   Traditionally, when developers address the issue of housing, they tend to deal with it as technocrats. They try to solve the problem by producing an amount of units, neglecting social issues and the complexity of the process. We want to be critical of the paradigm of architects and planners who believe that housing is simply about building units with space left over around them; spaces that remain empty and undifferentiated. Housing cannot simply be seen as "units," but must be embedded in an

Ulrike   Unsere Lage ist nicht deshalb schlecht, weil die Architektur schlecht wäre. Unsere Wohnungen sind komfortabel und wir möchten dort bleiben. Aber Wohnen hat auch eine ökonomische Dimension, wenn es darum geht, auf einem zunehmend neoliberalen Wohnungsmarkt seine Miete bezahlen zu können. Bei der Wohnungsfrage geht es nie nur um die Wohnungen selbst.

Melanie   Viele Probleme rund ums Wohnen sind von außen nicht erkennbar, zum Beispiel, wenn bis zu zehn Personen in einer Wohnung für nur eine Familie leben. Das sieht man von der Straße aus nicht. Das bleibt alles in den Wohnungen, wie auch die hohen Nebenkosten. Diese gelten für alle, betreffen die Leute aber abhängig von ihrer jeweiligen Situation auf unterschiedliche Art und Weise. In diesen Unterschieden liegt auch die Bedeutung des sozialen Wohnungsbaus.

Zehra   Als wir mit unserer Protestbewegung am Kotti begannen, dachte ich, das Problem sei auf Kreuzberg beschränkt. Es stellte sich aber schnell heraus, dass es die ganze Stadt betrifft – und nach ein paar bundesweiten Demonstrationen wurde mir klar, dass es dieses Problem im ganzen Land gibt. Und spätestens als wir euch kennengelernt haben, Teddy und Fonna, habe ich verstanden, dass es die ganze Welt betrifft. Die Politiker versuchen, das Wohnungsproblem zu vertuschen; es ist also an uns, es sichtbar zu machen.

Teddy   Üblicherweise gehen Bauunternehmer an die Wohnungsfrage heran wie Technokraten. Sie versuchen, das Problem über die Produktion einer bestimmten Anzahl von Wohneinheiten zu lösen, und vernachlässigen dabei soziale Aspekte und die Komplexität des Prozesses. Wir wollen kritisch an die Haltung von

Una conversación entre San Diego, Tijuana y Berlin

San Diego, Tijuana ve Berlin arasında bir sohbet

es

Con Teddy Cruz y Fonna Forman (Estudio Teddy Cruz + Forman), Ulrike Hamann, Melanie Dyck, Zehra Ulutürk, Alexander Sandy Kaltenborn, Fatma Cakmak y Angelika Levi (Kotti & Co), y Jesko Fezer (*Wohnungsfrage*)

tr

Teddy Cruz ve Fonna Forman (Estudio Teddy Cruz + Forman), Ulrike Hamann, Melanie Dyck, Zehra Ulutürk, Alexander Sandy Kaltenborn, Fatma Çakmak ve Angelika Levi (Kotti & Co) ile Jesko Fezer (*Wohnungsfrage*).

Ulrike Nuestra situación no es mala debido a la mala arquitectura. Disponemos de departamentos cómodos, los cuales queremos conservar, puesto que son nuestros hogares. Lo que nos importa es la dimensión económica de la vivienda, cómo pagar el alquiler dentro de un mercado de la vivienda cada vez más neoliberal. La vivienda no sólo tiene que ver con las casas en sí mismas.

Melanie Muchos de los temas en torno a la vivienda son invisibles desde el exterior. Por ejemplo, cuando viven hasta diez personas en un departamento unifamiliar. Esto no se ve desde la calle, permanece dentro de las viviendas, al igual que los altos precios de los servicios. Esto afecta a las personas de distinta manera según sus condiciones de vida. Estas diferencias determinan lo que realmente significa la vivienda de interés social.

Zehra Cuando comenzamos nuestro movimiento de protesta en el Kotti (forma coloquial de nombrar al Kottbusser Tor), pensé que este problema sólo existía en Kreuzberg. Pronto me di cuenta de que afecta a toda la ciudad y, tras unas cuantas manifestaciones, me quedó claro que el problema se puede encontrar en todo el país. Y ahora que hemos conocido a Teddy y Fonna es evidente que afecta a todo el mundo. Los políticos tratan de ocultar el problema de la vivienda. Por lo tanto, nos corresponde a nosotros hacerlo visible.

Teddy Tradicionalmente, cuando los promotores inmobiliarios abordan la cuestión de la vivienda, tienden a tratarla como tecnócratas. Tratan de resolver el problema mediante la producción de una cantidad de unidades, dejando de lado las cuestiones sociales y la complejidad del proceso. Somos críticos con el

Ulrike Durumumuzun kötü olmasının sebebi mimarinin kötülüğü değil. Evimiz olarak kullanmayı sürdürmek istediğimiz rahat konutlarımız var. Ancak konut meselesinin bir de ekonomik boyutu var yani giderek daha da neoliberalleşen konut pazarında kiraların nasıl ödeneceği. Konut meselesi asla sadece konutlarla ilgili bir konu değil.

Melanie Konut sorunuyla ilgili birçok konu dışarıdan görülemiyor, mesela tek bir ailenin yaşayabileceği bir konutta on kişinin yaşıyor olması. Bunu sokaktan göremeyiz. Bu binanın içinde kalan bir şey, tıpkı yüksek hizmet faturaları gibi. Bu durum herkes için geçerli fakat herkesi koşullarının çerçevesinde farklı etkiliyor. Sosyal konutlandırmanın gerçek anlamını belirleyen esasen bu ayrımlar.

Zehra Kotti'de protestoya başladığımızda bu sorunun sadece Kreuzberg'de olduğunu düşünüyordum. Kısa süre içinde tüm şehri ilgilendirdiğini anladım – ve birkaç ülke ölçeğinde eylemin ardından bu sorunun ülkenin her köşesinde görülebileceğini fark ettim. Teddy ve Fonna, sizleri tanımamla birlikte konunun tüm dünyayı ilgilendirdiğini net biçimde görmeye başladım. Politikacılar konut sorununun üzerini örtmeye çalışıyor; dolayısıyla görünür kılmak da bize kalmış.

Teddy Geleneksel olarak, kentsel gelişim uzmanları konut sorununa işaret ederken, konuya teknokrat gözüyle bakma eğilimindedirler. Belli sayıda birim üreterek, sosyal konuları ve sürecin karmaşıklığını yok sayarak sorunu çözmeye çalışırlar. Mimar ve şehir plancılarının, konut meselesini, çevresinde boş ve işlevlendirilmemiş alanlar bırakılmış bina ünitelerinden ibaret gören paradigması karşısında eleştirel

infrastructure of social, economic, and cultural support systems.

Fonna The challenge for us in this project is how to address the specific task of designing a housing model, producing something physical, how this integrates within the political agenda of Kotti & Co, and how that agenda can be elevated. The question at Kotti is not developing new prototypes of housing, but how to keep existing housing affordable for the people who live here. It became less about the units and more about the activity on the street, represented in the temporary, informal structure of the Gecekondu* itself, which you built here.

Ulrike Yes, the communality we have here only became fully apparent through this self-made building. It existed before, in parts, neighbors greeting and helping each other, children playing together. But it only became visible and really flourished when we squatted this public spot in front of our buildings.

Sandy It also brought along a strong exchange between different groups, diverse practices, and cultures in the neighborhood.

Jesko Through our conversations, I have learned how this place relates to the housing question. At first I had thought of this informal building *either* as a tool of visualization in your political struggle, *or* as an everyday meeting place in addition to people's private apartments. Now I realize that it is both. By taking the living room out onto the street, this neighborly space for communication has become the place of the political itself. How could this be transferred elsewhere?

Ulrike Our first goal was to make the problem of high rents in Berlin's social housing visible. It would not have been enough to stage a protest in front of the parliament only to disappear again the next day. We needed to be there permanently to remind the politicians of the problem. As we can see with the Gecekondu, this new structure is in need of a double functionality; it should enable the presence of protest on the street, but at the same time, it should protect this protest from the cold, rain, and noise. It should serve as a meeting point that can be both private and public.

Teddy What you have done here emphasizes that housing must be thought in relation to a different idea of public space. Before the Gecekondu, this was an empty space, but you inscribed inside that neutral space a very specific platform of sociability, knowledge, and exchange.

Architekten und Planern herangehen, die meinen, dass es beim Wohnungswesen nur um den Bau solcher Einheiten mit etwas Fläche darum herum geht – Räume, die leer und letztlich undefiniert bleiben. Wohnungen dürfen nicht einfach nur als „Einheiten" betrachtet werden, sondern müssen in eine funktionierende soziale, ökonomische und kulturelle Infrastruktur eingebettet sein.

Fonna Für uns besteht die Herausforderung bei diesem Projekt in der Frage, wie wir die konkrete Aufgabe für die Gestaltung eines Wohnmodells angehen, wie wir etwas Greifbares produzieren, wie sich das in die politische Agenda von Kotti & Co integrieren lässt und wie man die Agenda an sich in den Vordergrund rücken kann. Bei Kotti geht es nicht um die Entwicklung neuer Musterwohnungen, sondern um die Frage, wie der vorhandene Wohnraum für die Menschen, die hier leben, bezahlbar bleibt. Es ging weniger um die Wohneinheiten als um die Aktivitäten auf der Straße, die sich in der temporären, informellen Struktur des Gecekondus* manifestieren, das ihr hier errichtet habt.

Ulrike Ja, dass es hier ein Gemeinschaftsgefühl gibt, ist erst durch dieses selbstgebaute Haus deutlich geworden. Teilweise hat es das zwar schon vorher gegeben: Nachbarn, die sich gegenseitig grüßen und helfen, Kinder, die miteinander spielen. Aber es ist erst sichtbar geworden und in Schwung gekommen, als wir diesen öffentlichen Platz vor unseren Häusern in Beschlag genommen haben.

Sandy Darüber ist es auch zu einem intensiven Austausch zwischen verschiedenen Gruppen mit ihren diversen sozialen und kulturellen Praktiken gekommen.

Jesko Durch unsere Gespräche ist mir erst klar geworden, wie viel dieser Ort mit der Wohnungsfrage zu tun hat. Zuerst habe ich dieses „informelle" Haus als Werkzeug verstanden, um euren politischen Kampf sichtbar zu machen, oder als gern genutzten Treffpunkt außerhalb der Privatwohnung. Jetzt ist mir klar, dass es beides ist. Indem die Leute ihre Wohnzimmer quasi auf die Straße gebracht haben, ist dieser Nachbarschaftsraum selbst zum Ort des Politischen geworden. Wie könnte man das auf andere Orte übertragen?

Ulrike Unser Ziel war ursprünglich tatsächlich, das Problem der überhöhten Mieten im sozialen Wohnungsbau Berlins sichtbar zu machen. Es reicht nicht, eine Protestaktion vor dem Abgeordnetenhaus abzuhalten und dann wieder aus der öffentlichen Wahrnehmung zu verschwinden. Wir mussten andauernd präsent sein, um die Politiker an das Problem zu erinnern. Das Gecekondu muss also eine doppelte Funktion erfüllen: Es soll den Protest auf die Straße bringen, diesen Protest zugleich aber auch vor Kälte, Regen und

paradigma de los arquitectos y los planificadores, que creen que la vivienda es simplemente cuestión de construir unidades con un espacio sobrante alrededor de ellas, espacios que permanecen vacíos e indiferenciados. La vivienda no puede ser vista simplemente como "unidades", sino que debe estar integrada en una infraestructura de sistemas de apoyo social, económico y cultural.

Fonna   El desafío para nosotros en este proyecto es la manera de abordar la tarea específica de diseñar un modelo de vivienda. Producir algo físico que se pueda integrar a la agenda política de Kotti & Co, apoyando sus programas y actividades. Pero la cuestión para Kotti no es desarrollar nuevos prototipos de vivienda, sino cómo mantener asequible la vivienda existente para las personas que viven aquí. Es así como nuestra tarea se ha enfocado menos en una vivienda para el Kotti y más en apoyar su actividad en las calles, por medio de una estructura efímera, informal, expandiendo la capacidad del mismo Gecekondu* que ustedes construyeron aquí.

Ulrike   Sí, la comunidad que tenemos aquí sólo se hizo plenamente visible a través de este edificio auto construido. Aunque ya existía antes, en algunos lugares donde los vecinos se daban la bienvenida y se ayudaban los unos a los otros, y los niños jugaban juntos. Sin embargo, sólo se hizo visible y floreció verdaderamente cuando invadimos este lugar público frente a nuestros edificios.

Sandy   Esto también trajo consigo un fuerte intercambio entre los diferentes grupos, diversas prácticas y culturas en el barrio.

Jesko   A través de nuestras conversaciones, he comprendido cómo se relaciona este lugar con el problema de la vivienda. En un primer momento había pensado en este edificio informal como una herramienta de visualización en la lucha política de ustedes, o como un lugar de encuentro cotidiano, además de los departamentos privados de las personas. Ahora me doy cuenta de que es ambas cosas a la vez. Al sacar la sala de estar a la calle, este espacio vecinal de comunicación se ha convertido en el lugar de la política misma. ¿Cómo se puede transferir esto a otro lugar?

Ulrike   Nuestro primer objetivo es hacer visible el problema del alto costo de los alquileres de la vivienda social en Berlín. No habría sido suficiente escenificar una protesta frente al Parlamento para luego desaparecer al día siguiente. Teníamos que estar allí de forma permanente para recordar a los políticos sobre este problema. Como podemos ver con el Gecekondu, esta nueva estructura necesita una doble funcionalidad: debe permitir la presencia de manifestantes en la calle,

olmalıyız. Konut meselesi "ünite"lerden ibaret görülemez; sosyal, ekonomik ve kültürel destek sistemleri içeren bir altyapı üzerine bina edilmelidir.

Fonna   Bu projede karşı karşıya olduğumuz zorlu görev bir konutlandırma modeli kurma, fiziksel bir şey üretme işinin nasıl ele alınması gerektiği, ve bunu Kotti & Co'nun siyasal gündemi ile nasıl bütünleştirip bu gündemin nasıl yükseltileceği. Kotti'deki sorun yeni konut prototipleri geliştirmek değil, burada yaşayan insanlar için mevcut konut giderlerini karşılanabilir düzeyde tutmak. Burada inşa edilen Gecekondu'nun* geçici ve resmiyet kazanmayan yapısının ön plana çıkardığı şey binalardan ziyade sokak faaliyetleridir.

Gecekondu, Kottbusser Tor, Berlin

Ulrike   Evet, şu andaki ortaklaşmamızın tam anlamıyla belirgin hale gelmesi ancak bu kendi yaptığımız bina sayesinde oldu. Dayanışma kısmen daha önce de vardı, komşular birbirlerini selamlıyorlardı, yardımlaşıyorlardı ve çocuklar birlikte oynuyorlardı. Fakat görünür olması ve gerçek anlamda gelişmesi evlerimizin önündeki bu alana el koymamızla birlikte gerçekleşti.

Sandy   Aynı zamanda, farklı gruplar, çeşitli faaliyetler ve kültürler arasında güçlü bir alışverişi de beraberinde getirdi.

Jesko   Sohbetlerimiz sayesinde bu mekânın konut sorunuyla nasıl ilişkilendirileceğini de öğrendim. İlk başta bu informel binanın politik mücadelenizin görünür kılınmasını sağlayan bir araç ya da insanların özel konutlarına ek bir gündelik buluşma noktası olduğunu düşünüyordum. Şimdi anlıyorum ki her ikisi de doğru. Oturma odalarının sokağa taşınması, mahallelinin bu iletişim alanını tam bir politik mekâna dönüştürdü. Başka bir yerde bu dönüşüm nasıl sağlanabilirdi ki?

Sandy The Gecekondu is constantly transforming in relation to its social, cultural, and political usage, because different people with different kinds of knowledge built it. As for the referendum against high rents, when we collect signatures in front of the Gecekondu, it is a very communicative, activating tool. In other communities people want to participate in the referendum and start communicating more with their neighbors. Therefore, when we discuss and develop our architectural model for the Haus der Kulturen der Welt, we should always ask whether it would work for us as well as for other initiatives in this city.

Melanie For me, a mobile Gecekondu makes sense in the context of counseling. Other initiatives need support and solidarity. Just recently, we gave advice to three elderly men in Berlin-Reinickendorf, who cried, because they did not know what to do in their struggle for their homes. Maybe our 1:1 model could be useful temporarily in other parts of the city, too.

Fatma I think people must create it themselves in order to develop a relationship with it. This is the most important point. The Gecekondu exists because the neighborhood built it and everybody was part of the collective construction process. Some were building, while others were cleaning or cooking. Such a building would need the spirit of the neighborhood as part of the construction process so that the people own it emotionally. You cannot put this into a museum. What is specific, here, is that we added parts of our building over time; that it is open, transparent, with all its windows and doors, so that everybody can peer into it, enter, and sit down to drink tea.

Sandy At the beginning of the project, we were skeptical about whether we could create something transferable through spatial or architectural means. We do not think that much about physical objects, rather, we consider them from the perspective of their social meaning and usage; how they are embedded in our life and struggle. But when we think about a physical structure, multi-functionality becomes a must. Still, when we hand the model over for another group to use, this would not be enough. The existence of architectural structures does not guarantee that a similar social process will happen. A neighborhood does not simply exist, but has to be created, and remains precarious. Which elements could provoke what we do at Kotti somewhere else? Is a built structure even necessary? For instance, the samovar, as a social tool, is essential to our protest. Without the tea our protest wouldn't have happened.

Lärm schützen. Es soll als Treffpunkt dienen, der genauso öffentlich wie privat sein kann.

Teddy Was ihr hier gemacht habt, zeigt noch einmal deutlich, dass die Wohnungsfrage mit einer grundsätzlich anderen Vorstellung von öffentlichem Raum in Verbindung gebracht werden muss. Vor dem Bau des Gecekondu war dies ein leerer Platz, aber ihr habt aus diesem neutralen Raum eine ganz eigene Plattform für ein Miteinander, für Wissenserweiterung und Austausch gemacht.

Gecekondu, Kottbusser Tor, Berlin

Sandy Das Gecekondu verändert sich permanent mit seinen sozialen, kulturellen und politischen Nutzungen, auch weil es von unterschiedlichen Personen mit unterschiedlichem Hintergrundwissen gebaut wurde. Wenn wir vor dem Gecekondu Unterschriften für den Mietenvolksentscheid sammeln, erweist es sich als extrem kommunikatives und aktivierendes Werkzeug, das die Leute mobilisiert. Jetzt wollen sich auch Menschen in anderen Bezirken am Volksentscheid beteiligen und sich stärker mit ihren Nachbarn austauschen. Bei der Diskussion und der Entwicklung unseres Architekturmodells für das Haus der Kulturen der Welt sollten wir also immer auch die Frage im Hinterkopf behalten, ob es nicht nur für uns, sondern auch für andere Initiativen in dieser Stadt funktionieren würde.

Melanie Für mich macht ein mobiles Gecekondu Sinn, wenn es um den Zweck der Beratung geht. Andere Initiativen brauchen Unterstützung und Solidarität. Erst kürzlich haben wir drei ältere Männer in Berlin-Reinickendorf beraten, die um ihr Zuhause kämpfen. Sie mussten weinen, weil sie nicht wussten, was sie tun sollten. Vielleicht wäre unser 1:1-Modell zeitweise auch in anderen Teilen der Stadt nützlich.

pero al mismo tiempo debe proteger a dichos manifestantes contra el frío, la lluvia y el ruido. Debería servir como un punto de encuentro que pueda ser tanto público como privado.

Teddy   Lo que han hecho ustedes aquí destaca cómo debemos pensar la vivienda en relación a una idea diferente del espacio público. Antes del Gecekondu, este era un espacio vacío, pero ustedes inscribieron en ese espacio neutral una plataforma muy específica de sociabilidad, conocimiento e intercambio.

Sandy   El Gecekondu se está transformando constantemente en relación con su uso social, cultural y político, debido a que fue construido por personas con diferentes tipos de conocimiento. En cuanto al referéndum contra el alto costo del alquiler, el hecho de recoger firmas frente al Gecekondu ha sido una herramienta muy comunicativa y activadora. En otras comunidades las personas quieren participar en el referéndum y comienzan a comunicarse más con sus vecinos. Por lo tanto, cuando discutimos y desarrollamos nuestro modelo de arquitectura para la Haus der Kulturen der Welt, nos preguntamos si siempre funcionaría para nosotros igual que para otras iniciativas en esta ciudad.

Melanie   Para mí, un Gecekondu móvil tiene sentido en el contexto de la consejería. Otras iniciativas necesitan apoyo y solidaridad. Recientemente, dimos asesoramiento a tres ancianos en Berlin-Reinickendorf, que lloraban porque no sabían qué hacer en su lucha por sus hogares. Tal vez nuestro modelo 1:1 podría también ser útil temporalmente en otras partes de la ciudad.

Fatma   Creo que la gente debe crear su propio Gecekondu por sí misma para desarrollar una relación con él. Este es el punto más importante. El Gecekondu existe porque el barrio lo construyó, y todo el mundo formó parte del proceso de construcción colectiva. Algunos se ocupaban de la construcción, mientras otros limpiaban o cocinaban. Un edificio de este tipo tendría que tener el espíritu del barrio como parte del proceso de construcción, de tal forma que las personas se adueñen de él emocionalmente. No se puede poner esto en un museo. Lo que es específico, en este caso, es que hemos agregado partes de nuestro edificio a través del tiempo; que es abierto, transparente, con todas sus puertas y ventanas, para que todo el mundo pueda mirar dentro de él, entrar, sentarse y tomar té.

Sandy   Cuando iniciamos el proyecto, no creíamos que podríamos crear algo transferible a través de medios espaciales o arquitectónicos. No pensamos tanto en los objetos físicos, más bien los consideramos desde la perspectiva de su significado y su uso sociales, es decir

Ulrike   Birinci amacımız Berlin'deki yüksek sosyal konut kiraları sorununa dikkat çekmekti. Meclis binası önünde bir sonraki gün gözlerden uzaklaşacak bir protesto gösterisi sahnelemek yeterli değildi. Sorunu politikacılara hatırlatabilmek için süreklilik gerekiyordu. Gecekondu sayesinde görebileceğimiz gibi, bu yeni yapının ikili bir işlevi olması gerekiyordu; sokaklarda protestoyu mümkün kılmalı ama aynı zamanda bu protestoyu soğuktan, yağmurdan ve gürültüden de korumalıydı. Hem özel hem de kamusal bir buluşma noktası olmalıydı.

Teddy   Burada gerçekleştirdiğiniz şey konut sorununun farklı bir kamusal alan yaklaşımı ile birlikte düşünülmesi gerektiğini vurguluyor. Gecekondu'dan önce burası boş bir alandı ama siz bu boş alanda çok özel bir sosyalleşme, bilgi ve değişim platformu kurdunuz.

Sandy   Gecekondu, sosyal, kültürel ve siyasal kullanımına bağlı olarak sürekli dönüşüm yaşıyor zira onu farklı bilgi türlerine sahip farklı insanlar kurdu. Yüksek kiralarla ilgili referanduma gelecek olursak, önünde imza toplanırken Gecekondu iletişimsel, harekete geçirici bir araç haline geldi. Başka topluluklardan insanlar da referandumda yer almak ve kendi komşularıyla daha fazla iletişim kurmak istiyorlar. Dolayısıyla Haus der Kulturen der Welt için bir mimari modeli tartışırken ve tasarlarken, hem bize ve hem de şehirdeki diğer girişimlere hizmet etmesini sürekli göz önünde bulundurmamız gerekir.

Melanie   Bence, danışmanlık açısından seyyar bir Gecekondu anlamlı olacaktır. Diğer girişimlerin destek ve dayanışmaya gereksinimi var. Çok yakın bir zamanda, evleri için mücadele ederken ne yapmaları gerektiğini bilmediğinden yakınan Berlin-Reinickendorf'tan yaşlı üç adama tavsiyelerde bulunduk. Bire bir modelimiz belki şehrin diğer semtlerinde de geçici olarak faydalı olabilir.

Fatma   Sanırım onunla bir ilişki geliştirebilmek için insanlar onu kendileri yaratmalılar. En önemli nokta bu. Gecekondu'nun varlığını sağlayan mahallelilerce inşa edilmesi ve herkesin kolektif inşa sürecinin bir parçası olması. Bazıları doğrudan inşaatta çalışırken diğerleri temizlik yaptı ya da yemek pişirdi. Böyle bir binanın, inşa sürecinin bir parçası olarak mahallelilik ruhuna ihtiyacı var; böylelikle insanların ona duygusal anlamda sahip çıkması sağlanabilir. Bu ruh sergilenebilecek bir şey değil. Buraya özgü olan şey binamıza zaman içinde yeni eklemeler yapmış olmamız; herkes içeriye bakabilsin, girebilsin ve oturup bir çay içebilsin diye kapılarıyla, pencereleriyle açık ve şeffaf olması.

Ulrike   The structure itself does not impose the social use; the social practices shape the spatial designs. The same structure can be put to use somewhere else in a different way; it has to be flexible for a multitude of neighborhoods. The community will have to find out what is essential for them, which objects symbolize an inviting spirit, like our samovar here.

Fonna   If the structure exists, it can be adapted to the needs of the community. Through ordinary, daily social practices, the community becomes the architect. We think a lot about the roles of bottom-up social organization and top-down formal intervention, how do these dynamics converge? For example, infrastructures comprised of "housing parts" can enable easy distribution by non-governmental organizations, municipalities, and local activist groups, facilitating top-down support of bottom-up processes.

University of California, San Diego

Teddy   What we share with you is the discussion about informal urbanization. How bottom-up movements can inspire us to reorganize our ideas and conventions about housing. Another major point of contact between us is the notion of "retrofit." We see the Gecekondu as an act of retrofit into an undifferentiated public space, and most of our housing projects and processes on the United States–Mexican border are defined by adaptive and retrofitting strategies—whether we are working with the immigrant neighborhoods in San Diego or the informal settlements in Tijuana. There, materials, tires, and whole houses from across the border are recycled and reconfigured; garage doors become the new skin for informally built houses. How can we as architects intervene in those processes? These slums surround factories. Tijuana is considered a tax haven for multinationals. They take advantage of the slums for cheap labor without being accountable to the people

Fatma   Ich denke, die Leute sollten es selbst bauen, um dazu eine Beziehung zu entwickeln. Das ist das Wichtigste daran. Das Gecekondu existiert, weil die Leute hier es gemeinsam errichtet haben, alle waren Teil eines kollektiven Prozesses. Einige haben selbst mitgebaut, andere saubergemacht oder gekocht. Bei solch einem Bauwerk muss ein nachbarschaftlicher Geist mit von der Partie sein, damit die Leute das Gefühl haben, es gehört ihnen. So etwas kannst Du nicht auf einen Ausstellungsort übertragen. Das Besondere ist, dass unser Haus mit der Zeit gewachsen ist, dass es mit seinen vielen Fenstern und Türen offen und transparent ist. Jeder kann einen Blick hineinwerfen, kann hineingehen, kann sich hinsetzen, um einen Tee zu trinken.

Sandy   Zu Beginn des Projekts waren wir skeptisch, ob wir mit räumlichen beziehungsweise architektonischen Mitteln etwas schaffen könnten, das sich übertragen lässt. Wir denken eigentlich nicht so sehr an die Objekte selbst, sondern vielmehr an ihre soziale Bedeutung und Nutzung; wie sie sich in unser Leben und unseren politischen Kampf einfügen. Aber wenn wir nun über eine konkrete gegenständliche Struktur nachdenken, ist Multifunktionalität ein Muss. Das reicht aber nicht aus, wenn wir es zur Nutzung an eine andere Gruppe weitergeben wollten. Bauliche Strukturen sind noch keine Gewähr, dass ein vergleichbarer gesellschaftlicher Prozess anderswo stattfindet. Eine Nachbarschaft ist nicht einfach da, sie muss geschaffen werden und bleibt eine fragile Sache. Welche Elemente könnten das, was wir am Kotti gestaltet haben, anderswo entstehen lassen? Bedarf es überhaupt einer gebauten Struktur? Bei unserem Protest ist beispielsweise der Samowar als soziales Instrument von großer Bedeutung. Ohne Tee hätte unser Protest nie stattgefunden.

Ulrike   Die gesellschaftliche Nutzung ergibt sich nicht aus dem Gebäude selbst; das räumliche Design wird von den sozialen Praktiken bestimmt. Das gleiche Haus lässt sich anderswo anders nutzen; es muss für viele verschiedene Nachbarschaften flexibel sein. Die jeweilige Gemeinschaft muss herausfinden, was ihr wichtig ist, welche Dinge jeweils etwas Einladendes darstellen, so wie unser Samowar.

Fonna   Ist eine Struktur vorhanden, kann sie an die Anforderungen der Community angepasst werden. Gewöhnliche, alltägliche soziale Gewohnheiten machen die Gemeinschaft zum Architekten. Wir denken viel über die Bedeutung der sozialen Organisation von unten und der formellen Intervention von oben nach, darüber, wie sich diese Dynamiken einander annähern können. So können Infrastrukturelemente, die aus „Wohn-Teilen" bestehen, eine reibungslose Verteilung über gemeinnützige Organisationen, städtische Kommunen und lokale Aktionsgruppen ermöglichen und

la manera en que están integrados en nuestras vidas y nuestra lucha. Pero, cuando pensamos en una estructura física, la funcionalidad múltiple se convierte en un requisito. Aun así, cuando le damos el modelo a otro grupo para que lo utilice, esto no sería suficiente. La existencia de estructuras arquitectónicas no garantiza que vaya a darse un proceso social similar. El sentimiento de vecindad no sólo existe, sino que tiene que ser creado, y aún así sigue siendo precario. ¿Qué elementos podrían provocar lo que hacemos en Kotti en algún otro lugar? ¿Es incluso necesaria una estructura construida? Por ejemplo, el samovar, como herramienta social, es esencial para nuestra protesta. Sin el té nuestra protesta no se hubiera llevado a cabo.

Ulrike   La estructura en sí misma no impone el uso social. Las prácticas sociales dan forma a los diseños espaciales. La misma estructura se puede utilizar en otro lugar de forma diferente, tiene que ser flexible para muchos vecindarios. La comunidad tendrá que averiguar lo que es esencial para ellos, qué objetos simbolizan un espíritu acogedor, como sucede aquí con nuestro samovar.

Fonna   Si la estructura existe, ésta puede ser adaptada a las necesidades de la comunidad. Mediante prácticas sociales ordinarias, cotidianas, la comunidad se convierte en una suerte de arquitecto. Pensamos mucho sobre las funciones de la organización social desde abajo hacia arriba y en la intervención formal de arriba hacia abajo. Pero, ¿cómo convergen estas dinámicas? Por ejemplo, las infraestructuras compuestas de "piezas de vivienda" pueden permitir una distribución sencilla por parte de las organizaciones no gubernamentales, municipios y grupos de activistas locales, mostrando cómo un sistema formal desde arriba hacia abajo puede facilitar los procesos sociales de abajo.

Teddy   Lo que compartimos con ustedes es una discusión sobre la urbanización informal y cómo los movimientos de abajo hacia arriba nos pueden inspirar para reorganizar nuestras ideas y convenciones en materia de vivienda. Otro importante punto de contacto entre nosotros es el concepto de "adaptación urbana". Podemos ver al Gecekondu como un acto de adaptación de un espacio público indiferenciado, y la mayoría de nuestros proyectos y procesos de vivienda en la frontera entre Estados Unidos y México se definen por estrategias de adaptación urbana –ya sea a través de proyectos en los barrios de inmigrantes en San Diego o en los asentamientos informales en Tijuana. En estos asentamientos podemos ver, por ejemplo, cómo los materiales y desechos urbanos de San Diego, las llantas y las viejas casas de posguerra de esa ciudad se trasladan a Tijuana, se reciclan y se reconfiguran, y cómo las puertas de garaje se convierten en la nueva piel de

Sandy   Projenin başlangıcında mekânsal ya da mimari araçlarla dönüştürülebilir bir şey yaratabileceğimiz konusunda kuşkularımız vardı. Fiziksel objelerden ziyade onların toplumsal anlamları ve kullanımları perspektifinden bakıyoruz; hayatımıza ve mücadelemize nasıl dâhil olduklarıyla ilgiliyiz. Ancak fiziksel bir yapı üzerine düşündüğümüzde çok-işlevlilik zorunluluk haline geliyor. Yine de, modeli başka bir grubun kullanımına sunduğumuzda bu yeterli olmayacaktır. Mimari yapıların varlığı her yerde benzer bir toplumsal sürecin işleyeceğinin teminatı değildir. Mahallelilik kendiliğinden var olmaz, yaratılmalıdır ve kararsız bir seyir izleyecektir. Bizim Kotti'de yaptığımızı başka bir yerde de harekete geçirecek unsurlar nelerdir? İnşa edilmiş bir yapı gerçekten gerekli midir? Mesela bizim mücadelemizde bir sosyal araç olarak semaver hayati önemdeydi. Çay olmadan protestomuz gerçekleşemezdi.

Ulrike   Yapının kendisi sosyal kullanımı dayatmaz; mekânsal tasarımları şekillendiren toplumsal pratiklerdir. Aynı yapı başka bir yerde farklı biçimde kullanılabilir; mahallelilik olgusunun çeşitliliği nedeniyle böylesi yapılar esnek olmalıdır. Kendileri için hayati olanın ne olduğunu, bizim semaverimiz gibi davetkâr bir ruhu sembolize edecek objelerinin neler olabileceğini topluluk kendisi bulmalıdır.

Fonna   Eğer yapı mevcutsa topluluğun gereksinimlerine uyarlanabilir. Olağan, gündelik toplumsal pratikler aracılığıyla topluluk sürecin mimarı olur. Aşağıdan yukarıya toplumsal örgütlenme ve yukarıdan aşağıya resmi müdahalenin rolleri hakkında çok kafa yoruyoruz, bu dinamikler nasıl kesişiyor? Mesela, "yerleşim bölümleri"nin oluşturduğu altyapı sivil toplum kuruluşları, yerel yönetimler, yerel aktivist gruplar tarafından paylaşılarak aşağıdan yukarıya süreçlere yukarıdan aşağıya desteği kolaylaştırır.

Teddy   Sizlerle paylaştığımız şeylerden biri informel kentleşme yaklaşımı. Aşağıdan yukarıya hareketler konutlandırma konusundaki düşünce ve alışkanlıklarımızı yeniden kurgulamamız açısından bize nasıl esin kaynağı oluyor. Diğer önemli bir temas noktamız "tadilat" kavramı. Gecekondu'yu, işlevlendirilmemiş kamusal alanda bir tadilat girişimi olarak görüyoruz ve Birleşik Devletler-Meksika sınırındaki konutlandırma projeleri ve süreçleri de uyarlama ve tadilat stratejileri ile tanımlanıyor – ister San Diego'daki göçmen mahalleleriyle ister Tijuana'daki informel yerleşimlerle çalışıyor olalım. Orada, sınırın ötesinden getirilen malzeme, araba lastikleri ve komple evler geri kazanılıyor ve yeniden şekillendiriliyor; garaj kapıları informel olarak inşa edilen evlerin yeni dış yüzeyi haline geliyor. Mimar olarak bizler bu sürece nasıl katılabiliriz? Bu derme çatma yapılar fabrikaları çevreliyor. Tijuana çokuluslu

living in them. We decided to ask one of these factories for materials that can make the recycling of houses a lot safer. Instead of building new houses, we inject small infrastructures, because people there are already building houses themselves although the existing houses are often unstable. We then started thinking about architecture, not as houses, but as a series of parts that can inject themselves into the environment. We want to give the informal the tools to begin a process of formalization, to retrofit housing with social and material support systems.

Colonia Libertad, Tijuana

Ulrike   Many here can relate easily to the situation at the border you describe. First, because the conditions of migration and the divisions that borders create are inherent in the knowledge of our neighborhood. We all know of community gardens and other informal uses of common spaces in Berlin, although we may not talk about it in such terms. On the other hand, we have to deal with an extremely formalized urban space here. Even though the informal continues to emerge—and Kreuzberg has always been the place for the highest possible informality with its history of squatting and self-organized gardens—in Germany, we have a very strictly regulated use of public space. If for instance we wanted to organize a collective *Iftar*—the dinner during Ramadan—as a neighborhood event on the street, we would have to apply four months in advance and four to five district departments would have to approve the application. That we have kept an informal structure like our Gecekondu alive here for three years now is a miracle.

Fonna   Thinking about the relationship between these two sites—the concrete visual formality of Kottbusser Tor and the explosive volatility of the informal Tijuana slum—a powerful narrative emerges about what these sites can learn from each other and

so die Unterstützung von oben für Prozesse von unten vereinfachen.

Teddy   Was uns mit euch verbindet, ist die Diskussion über eine Stadtentwicklung, die nicht von oben gesteuert ist. Wie Bewegungen von unten uns dazu motivieren, unsere Vorstellungen und Konventionen in punkto Wohnen neu zu ordnen. Eine weitere wichtige Gemeinsamkeit ist die Idee des „Retrofit". Wir betrachten das Gecekondu als Akt der Nachrüstung eines noch nicht final definierten öffentlichen Raumes, wie auch die meisten unserer Wohnprojekte an der Grenze zwischen den USA und Mexiko durch Strategien von Anpassung und Umbau geprägt sind – ob wir nun mit den Einwanderervierteln in San Diego oder den informellen Siedlungen in Tijuana arbeiten. Dort werden Materialien, Reifen und ganze Häuser von der anderen Seite der Grenze recycelt und umgestaltet; Garagentüren werden zur neuen Außenhaut der inoffiziell errichteten Häuser. Wie können wir uns als Architekten in diese Prozesse einbringen? Diese Slums entstehen in der Umgebung von Fabriken. Tijuana gilt als Steueroase für multinationale Konzerne. Sie profitieren von den billigen Arbeitskräften in den Slums, ohne für die Menschen, die dort leben, Verantwortung zu übernehmen. Wir haben uns daher entschlossen, eine dieser Fabriken um Materialien zu bitten, mit denen sich die recycelten Häuser stabiler machen lassen. Statt neue Häuser zu bauen, bringen wir kleine infrastrukturelle „Injektionen" ein, denn die Leute vor Ort bauen ihre Häuser ohnehin selbst, aber es sind eben häufig ziemlich wackelige Konstruktionen. Dann haben wir angefangen, über Architektur nachzudenken, nicht in Form ganzer Häuser, sondern als eine Serie von Teilen, die in die bereits vorhandene Umgebung eingepasst werden können. Wir wollten dem, was informell gewachsen war, Werkzeuge an die Hand geben, um einen Verstetigungsprozess einzuleiten, um Wohngebäude mit Retrofit-Systemen sozial und materiell nachzurüsten.

Ulrike   Viele hier können die von dir beschriebene Situation gut nachvollziehen. Zum einen, weil sie mit den Lebensumständen der Migration und der Spaltung, die eine Grenze hervorbringt, aus eigener Anschauung vertraut sind. Wir alle kennen informelle Gärten und andere informelle Nutzungen öffentlicher Räume in Berlin, auch wenn wir vielleicht andere Begriffe benutzen würden. Andererseits haben wir es hier mit einem extrem formalisierten urbanen Raum zu tun. Auch wenn immer mehr Informelles entsteht – und Kreuzberg mit seiner Geschichte der Hausbesetzungen und den selbstorganisierten Gärten war schon immer ein Ort größtmöglicher Informalität –, ist die Nutzung des öffentlichen Raums in der Bundesrepublik stark reglementiert. Um beispielsweise ein gemeinsames *Iftar* – das Fastenbrechen während des Ramadan

las casas construidas de manera informal. ¿Cómo podemos los arquitectos intervenir en estos procesos? Al mismo tiempo, estos tugurios se encuentran alrededor de las fábricas. Tijuana es considerada un paraíso fiscal para las empresas multinacionales. Aprovechan la mano de obra barata de los asentamientos informales sin hacerse responsables de las personas que viven en ellos. Decidimos acercarnos a una de estas fábricas para pedir materiales que puedan hacer que el reciclaje de viviendas y desechos sea mucho más seguro. En lugar de construir nuevas casas, inyectamos pequeñas infraestructuras para apoyar el proceso de autoconstrucción, ya que la gente allí está construyendo sus propias viviendas, pero suelen ser bastante inestables. Es así como empezamos a pensar en la arquitectura, no como casas enteras, sino como una serie de piezas que se introducen en el medio ambiente existente. Queremos darle a lo informal las herramientas para iniciar un proceso de formalización, adaptando a la vivienda con sistemas de apoyo social y material.

Ulrike   Muchos de los que estamos aquí podemos relacionarnos fácilmente con la situación que ustedes describen de la frontera. En primer lugar, porque las condiciones de migración y las divisiones que crean las fronteras son inherentes al conocimiento de nuestro barrio. Todos conocemos los jardines y otros usos informales de los espacios comunes en Berlín, aunque no hablemos de ellos en esos términos. Por otro lado, aquí tenemos que lidiar con un espacio urbano extremadamente formalizado. A pesar de que lo informal sigue apareciendo –y Kreuzberg siempre ha sido un lugar de mucha informalidad con su historia de ocupaciones ilegales y de jardines auto organizados–, en Alemania tenemos un uso del suelo estrictamente regulado hacia el espacio público. Si, por ejemplo, quisiéramos organizar un *Iftar* colectivo –la cena durante el mes de Ramadán– como un evento de barrio en la calle, tendríamos que hacer la solicitud con cuatro meses de anticipación, y cuatro a cinco departamentos gubernamentales del distrito tendrían que aprobar la solicitud. El que hayamos mantenido viva una estructura informal como nuestro Gecekondu desde hace tres años es un milagro.

Fonna   Pensando en la relación entre estos dos sitios –la formalidad visual concreta del Kottbusser Tor y la volatilidad explosiva del asentamiento informal de Tijuana– , surge una potente narrativa sobre lo que estos sitios pueden aprender los unos de los otros y también hay una interesante correspondencia entre la relación formal e informal en ambos. En la forma concreta del proyecto de construcción urbana, lo que se entiende por la "ciudad oficial", hay sensibilidades sociales y económicas informales emergentes que necesitan ser amplificadas. Esto es lo que ejemplifica el Gecekondu. En la informalidad tugurio-urbana de

şirketler için vergi cenneti addediliyor. İçlerinde yaşayanlara karşı hiçbir sorumluluk taşımadan bu derme çatma evlerin ucuz emeğinden yararlanıyorlar. Bu fabrikaların birinden, evlerin geri kazanımını çok daha güvenle yapmayı sağlayacak malzeme istemeye karar verdik. Yeni evler inşa etmek yerine küçük altyapısal birimler ekliyoruz zira - her ne kadar mevcut evler sağlam olmasa da – oradaki insanlar zaten evlerini inşa ediyorlar. Daha sonra mimariyi düşünmeye başladık; evler olarak değil de çevreye kendiliğinden eklenebilecek bir dizi birim olarak. Amacımız informel olana formelleşme sürecini başlatacak araçları sunmak, konutları sosyal yardımlaşma ve malzeme desteği sistemleri ile tadil etmek.

Tijuana

Ulrike   Anlattığınız sınırdaki durumla buradaki birçok insan kolayca ilişkilendirilebilir. Birincisi, göç koşulları ve sınırların yarattığı bölünme mahallemizdeki insanların deneyim dağarcığında mevcut. Her ne kadar aynı kavramlarla ifade etmesek de Berlin'deki informel bahçeleri ve ortak alanların diğer informel kullanılma biçimlerini hepimiz biliyoruz. Diğer yandan, burada aşırı derecede formelleşmiş bir kentsel alan kullanımıyla baş etmek zorundayız. Informel oluşum Almanya'da yükselişini sürdürse de - ayrıca Kreuzberg, gecekondu ve mahalleli girişimiyle kurulan bahçeler geçmişiyle, mümkün olan en yüksek informelliğin olduğu semttir - kamusal alan kullanımı sıkı bir denetim altındadır. Örneğin mahallede bir sokak faaliyeti olarak kolektif İftar - Ramazan ayında yenilen akşam yemekleri - düzenlemek istesek dört ay önce başvuru yapmamız ve dört ya da beş yerel kurumun izni gerekir. Bizim Gecekondu gibi informel bir yapının üç yıldır yaşıyor olması bir mucize.

Fonna   Bu iki yerleşim arasındaki ilişki düşünüldüğünde – Kottbusser Tor'un somut bariz formelliği

there is also an interesting correspondence about the relation of the formal and informal in each of them. Within the concrete form of the urban housing project, the "official city," there are emergent informal social and economic sensibilities that need to be scaled-up, which the Gecekondu exemplifies. Within the urban-slum informality of Tijuana, the "unofficial city," there needs to be formal systems to support the evolutionary housing processes with an infrastructure of retrofit. This double project of retrofit—the informal into the formal and the formal into the informal—can be an organizing conceptual framework for our story of collaboration. In both cases, the deployment of material and spatial systems depends on social organization.

Teddy The main agenda in Kotti & Co's activist work is to advance processes that push the state to take accountability for rent control; in essence, to lower rents and enable subsidy structures that are just and sustainable. You enable new community-engaged knowledge from the bottom-up to produce a new affordable-housing agenda. This coincides with our research at the US–Mexican border that engages new processes to visualize the hidden development tools, across private and public protocols and mechanisms, to make affordable housing possible.

Angelika When we try to bring the issue of affordable housing into the museum, it has to be a provocation to an audience that does not necessarily know about the problems of social housing; visitors are not likely to be affected by the social and economic conditions we face here. How can we transport our context to this space: the questions of how the "Jobcenter," the employment office, treats us, the questions of economics? The housing question involves the possibility of eviction. For this, we would need the architectural structure also to be a shelter.

Jesko Indeed. But housing is not only about shelter. What is required is to reclaim those spaces around housing, which can be spaces of local productivity as well as social encounter, spaces that enable tenants to improve their own lives practically and to have a say in the planning of housing in the future and in the modification of the status quo.

Teddy Another way to address economic issues could be by making the hub an economic incubator, emphasizing that the issue of affordable rents is inherent to the issue of generating jobs. I imagine small businesses in many apartments here, people producing things. The hub could foster these, connecting this level of productivity in the private space, to the street.

– als Nachbarschaftsevent auf der Straße zu veranstalten, müssten wir vier Monate vorher einen Antrag stellen und vier bis fünf Ämter müssten diesen Antrag genehmigen. Dass es uns gelungen ist, ein informelles Gebäude wie das Gecekondu hier seit drei Jahren am Leben zu erhalten, grenzt an ein Wunder.

Fonna Denkt man über die Beziehung zwischen diesen beiden Orten nach – der soliden visuellen Gestalt des Kottbusser Tors und der explosiven Unbeständigkeit des informellen Slums in Tijuana –, zeigt uns das sehr eindrücklich, was die beiden Orte voneinander lernen können. Es besteht eine interessante Übereinstimmung, was die Beziehung zwischen dem Formellen und dem Informellen in den jeweiligen Projekten angeht. Innerhalb der konkreten Form der Wohnsiedlung, der „offiziellen Stadt", sehen wir die Entwicklung eines neuen informellen und ökonomischen Bewusstseins, das ausgebaut werden muss, und für das das Gecekondu ein gutes Beispiel ist. Innerhalb des informellen Slums in Tijuana, der „inoffiziellen Stadt", werden formelle Systeme benötigt, um die Bauprozesse mit einer funktionierenden Infrastruktur auszustatten. Diese doppelte Nachrüstung – des Formellen mit dem Informellen und des Informellen mit dem Formellen – kann einen konzeptuellen Rahmen für unsere Zusammenarbeit bilden. In beiden Fällen hängt die Bereitstellung materieller und räumlicher Systeme von der gesellschaftlichen Organisationsform ab.

Teddy Das Hauptanliegen der Aktionen von Kotti & Co besteht darin, Prozesse anzustoßen, die den Staat dazu bringen, bei der Mietpreiskontrolle Verantwortung zu übernehmen; im Wesentlichen, die Mieten zu senken und gerechte und nachhaltige Beihilfestrukturen zu ermöglichen. Ihr fördert ein neuartiges, gemeinschaftlich entwickeltes Wissen von unten, um eine Agenda für bezahlbares Wohnen zu schaffen. Das deckt sich mit unseren Recherchen an der US-amerikanisch-mexikanischen Grenze, bei denen wir uns neuer Strategien bedienen, um anhand privater wie öffentlicher Normen und Mechanismen Entwicklungsinstrumente sichtbar zu machen, mit denen sich Wohnen bezahlbar machen lässt.

Angelika Wenn wir versuchen wollen, das Problem bezahlbaren Wohnens an einen Ausstellungsort zu bringen, dann mittels einer Provokation, die sich an das Publikum richtet, das die Probleme des sozialen Wohnungsbaus nicht unbedingt kennt. Die Ausstellungsbesucher sind mit großer Wahrscheinlichkeit von den sozialen und wirtschaftlichen Bedingungen, die wir hier erleben, nicht betroffen. Wie können wir unsere Lebensumstände in diesen Raum übertragen: die Frage, wie das Jobcenter uns behandelt, unsere wirtschaftlichen Probleme? Zur Wohnungsfrage gehört auch das Thema Zwangsräumung. Deshalb sollte

Tijuana, es decir la ciudad "no oficial", tiene que haber sistemas formales de apoyo para los procesos de vivienda en evolución, con una infraestructura de adaptación. Este doble proyecto de adaptación –lo informal dentro de lo formal y lo formal dentro de lo informal– puede ser un marco conceptual organizativo para nuestra historia de colaboración. En ambos casos, el despliegue de sistemas materiales y espaciales depende de la organización social.

Gecekondu, Kottbusser Tor, Berlin

Teddy El programa principal de trabajo de los activistas de Kotti & Co es impulsar procesos que lleven al Estado a tomar la responsabilidad de controlar la fluctuación de los alquileres. En esencia, no permitir el aumento de los alquileres y posibilitar estructuras de subsidio que sean justas y sostenibles. Ustedes hacen posible que el conocimiento de base comunitaria se consolide para crear una nueva agenda de vivienda asequible. Esto coincide con nuestra investigación en la frontera México-EEUU por medio de la cual hemos abierto nuevos procesos para visualizar herramientas de desarrollo que suelen estar ocultas, a través de protocolos y mecanismos públicos y privados, para hacer posible la vivienda de bajo costo.

Angelika Cuando intentamos llevar el tema de la vivienda asequible al museo, esto tiene que haber sido una provocación para un público que no necesariamente sabe acerca de los problemas de la vivienda social, puesto que puede ser que los visitantes no sean del tipo a los que afectan las condiciones sociales y económicas que enfrentamos aquí. Pero, ¿cómo podemos transportar nuestro contexto a este espacio: las cuestiones sobre cómo nos trata la oficina de empleo, o el tema económico? La cuestión de la vivienda supone la posibilidad del desalojo. Para ello necesitaríamos que la estructura arquitectónica fuera también un refugio.

ile informel Tijuana yoksul yerleşiminin patlamaya hazır oynak zemini – birbirlerinden neler öğrenebileceklerine dair güçlü bir anlatı ortaya çıkıyor. Ayrıca her ikisindeki formelliğin ve informelliğin ilişkisiyle ilgili olarak da ilginç bir tekabüliyet var. Kentsel konutlandırma projesinde, "resmî kent"in somut biçimi içinde, geliştirilmesi gereken informel sosyal ve ekonomik hassasiyetler filizleniyor ki Gecokondu buna örnek teşkil ediyor. "Resmi olmayan kent" Tijuana'nın kentsel yoksul mahalle informelliğinde, gelişimsel konutlandırma süreçlerinin tadil edilmiş altyapı ile desteklenebilmesi için formel sistemlere gerek var. Bu ikili tadil projesi – formel olanın informele ve informel olanın formele – bizim işbirliği hikâyemiz için kavramsal bir çerçeve oluşturabilir. Her iki vakada da maddi ve mekânsal sistemlerin konumlanışı sosyal organizasyonlara dayanıyor.

Teddy Kotti & Co aktivist çalışmasının asli gündemi, kiraların denetimi için devleti sorumluluk almaya itecek süreçlerin geliştirilmesi; özü itibarıyla, kiraların düşürülmesi ile adil ve sürdürülebilir destek yapılarının mümkün hale getirilmesi. Aşağıdan yukarı, topluluk-odaklı yeni düşünceye yeni bir karşılanabilir konutlandırma gündemi üretme imkanı tanıyorsunuz. Bu durum, ödenebilir konutlandırmayı mümkün kılabilmek için özel ve kamusal protokol ve mekanizmalar arasındaki örtük gelişimsel araçları görünür kılmaya yönelik yeni süreçlere odaklanan Birleşik Devletler-Meksika sınırındaki araştırmamızla çakışıyor.

Angelika Karşılanabilir konutlandırma meselesini sergi mekanında kamuoyuna sunmak istiyorsak, bu sosyal konutlandırmanın sorunlarına dair hiçbir şey bilmeyebilecek olan gözlemciler için kışkırtıcı olmalı; ziyaretçiler burada karşılaştığımız sosyal ve ekonomik koşullardan etkilenmemiş olabilirler. Bağlamımızı bu alana nasıl aktarabiliriz: "Jobcenter"in, istihdam ofisinin bize karşı tutumunun yarattığı sorunları, ekonominin sorunlarını? Konut sorunu tahliye ihtimalini de içeriyor. Bu nedenle, mimari yapının aynı zamanda barınak olmasına da ihtiyacımız var.

Jesko Tabii ki. Ama konutlandırma sadece barınmayla sınırlı değil. Gerekli olan konutların çevresindeki alanların talep edilmesi. Bu alanlar hem yerel üretkenlik ve hem de sosyal temas mekânları haline gelebilir, semt sakinlerinin kendi yaşamlarını fiilen geliştirmelerini, gelecekteki konutlandırma planlamalarında ve statükonun değiştirilmesinde söz sahibi olmalarını sağlayabilir.

Teddy Ekonomik konulara değinmenin bir diğer yolu, karşılanabilir kira meselesinin iş imkânları yaratılması konusunda içkin olduğunu vurgulayarak bu merkezi bir ekonomik kuluçka makinesine çevirmek

Jesko   Es cierto. Pero la vivienda no es sólo una cuestión de refugio. Lo que se necesita es recuperar esos espacios alrededor de las viviendas, que pueden ser espacios de productividad local, así como de encuentro social, espacios que permiten a los inquilinos mejorar sus propias vidas de forma práctica y tener una voz en la planificación del futuro de la vivienda y en la modificación del status quo.

Teddy   Otra forma de abordar las cuestiones económicas sería que el centro de actividades fuera una incubadora económica, haciendo hincapié en que la cuestión de los alquileres asequibles es inherente a la cuestión de la creación de empleo. Me imagino que ya existen pequeñas empresas en muchos de los departamentos aquí, personas que producen cosas dentro de las viviendas. La estructura arquitectónica, como centro de actividades, puede promover estas empresas, conectando la productividad en el espacio privado con la calle.

Sandy   Muchas de las economías de los inmigrantes aquí son familiares. Son una mezcla de organización formal e informal del trabajo, sin distinción entre la esfera privada y la pública. Esta perspectiva también se refleja en nuestra comprensión de la economía, que va más allá de lo que se considera "trabajo" en el sentido clásico.

Ulrike   Para sacar algunas conclusiones de nuestros debates sobre el modelo 1:1, pienso que necesitamos una estructura arquitectónica que sea flexible en su uso y que también pueda migrar a otros barrios para que realicen allí sus reuniones y protestas. Sin embargo, no sólo debe ser un centro de actividades para la protesta política y la adquisición de información, sino también un espacio social, un espacio de protección como refugio, y para la dimensión económica de la vivienda y de la protesta, por ejemplo a través de la venta de alimentos o productos caseros.

Teddy   Estamos muy entusiasmados con la idea de una "estación" ligera y flexible que puede ocupar un espacio vacío en el barrio. Asimismo, nos interesa apoyar una nueva actividad económica en pequeña escala que surja de las prácticas cotidianas y de las relaciones sociales entre los inquilinos. Esto podría conectar la falta de acceso a la vivienda con las cuestiones del desempleo. Esto no va en contra del argumento que Kotti & Co ha estado defendiendo – bajar el precio de los alquileres y mantenerlo estable. Sin embargo, además de esta premisa, que requiere de la responsabilidad del Estado, es decir 'de arriba hacia abajo', nosotros afirmamos que la vivienda debe permitir las sensibilidades y capacidades de abajo hacia arriba para promover una creatividad económica que beneficie a los inquilinos. La urgente necesidad de establecer esta conexión entre los espacios de productividad local y las unidades de

olabilir. Buradaki evlerde birçok küçük iş yapıldığını, insanların bir şeyler ürettiklerini hayal ediyorum. Merkez, özel alandaki bu üretkenlik düzeyini sokakla bağlantılandırarak geliştirebilir.

Sandy   Burada göçmenlerin ekonomik faaliyetleri bir çoğu ailelerce yürütülüyor. Özel ve kamusal alan ayrımı yapılmaksızın, resmi ve gayri-resmî işgücü bileşenlerinden oluşuyorlar. Bu bakış açısı, klasik anlamda "iş"in ötesine geçen ekonomi anlayışımızda da yansıması buluyor.

San Diego

Ulrike   Bire bir model üzerine tartışmalarımızdan varılacak sonuçlara gelecek olursak, bence hem esnek işlevli hem de toplantı ve protestolarda kullanılmak üzere farklı mahallelere götürülebilen mimari yapılara ihtiyacımız var. Ancak sadece siyasal protesto ve bilgi merkezi olarak çalışmamalı, aynı zamanda hem sosyal mekân hem de bir koruyucu mekân, bir barınak olmalı ve konutlandırma ve protestonun ekonomik boyutuna da merkezlik etmeli – yiyecek ya da ev yapımı ürünler satılmalı.

Teddy   Mahallede belli bir boş alanı işgal edecek hafif, esnek bir "merkez"in varlığı ve bu merkezin kiracılar arasındaki gündelik pratiklerden ve sosyal ilişkilerden türeyen küçük ölçekli ekonomik faaliyetleri desteklemesi düşüncesi bizi heyecanlandırıyor. Bu durum potansiyel olarak kirayı karşılama gücünden yoksunluk ile işsizlik sorunlarını bağlantılandırabilir. Bu, Kotti & Co'nun mücadelesini verdiği tezlerin – kiraların düşürülmesi ve güvence altına alınması – önünü kesmez ama bu önermeye ek olarak, biz devletin, yukarıdan aşağıya sorumluluğunun dışında konut sorununun aşağıdan yukarıya hassasiyetini ve kiracıların yararlanabileceği ekonomik yaratıcılık kapasitesini de harekete geçirmesi gerektiğini savunuyoruz. Yerel üretkenlik mekânı ve konut birimleri arasındaki bu bağlantının acilen kurulması

Sandy *Wohnungsfrage* put Kotti & Co in the position to commission an architect. The outcome has not been either architectonic or spatial, in the sense of a new design for the social housing of the future. Instead, you took into account that we operate in a very specific setting. The result is not a housing unit, but a flexible, modular tool to enable neighborhoods to start communicating in the first place. Such a proposal extends the housing question. When we talk about housing, we also think about neighborhoods and the social fabric, which includes economies, political conditions, and so on. However, we probably have not found a properly architectonic solution to the question that is posed here, as the solution for social housing is primarily political.

Übernahme von Verantwortung seitens des Staates Wohnen auf eine Art stattfinden muss, die offen ist für Belange von unten und Kapazitäten für eine den Mietern zugutekommende wirtschaftliche Kreativität schafft. Die Dringlichkeit dieser Verbindung zwischen lokalem Gewerbe und dem Wohnungswesen ist kein auf Berlin beschränktes Phänomen; diese Verbindung ist überall erforderlich, insbesondere wenn über öffentlichen Wohnungsbau nachgedacht wird. Der öffentliche Wohnungsbau ist heute nicht mehr tragbar ohne eine stabilisierende Infrastruktur, die von sozialen und ökonomischen Systemen durchzogen ist.

Sandy *Wohnungsfrage* hat Kotti & Co in die Position gebracht, einen Architekten zu beauftragen. Das Ergebnis ist weder eine architektonische noch ein räumliche Lösung im Sinne eines Neuentwurfs für den sozialen Wohnungsbau der Zukunft. Stattdessen hast du als Architekt unsere ganz speziellen Lebenszusammenhänge berücksichtigt. Das Resultat ist keine Wohneinheit, sondern ein flexibles, modulares Instrument, welches den Menschen eines Viertels die Möglichkeit gibt, miteinander ins Gespräch zu kommen. Ein derartiger Entwurf geht über die Wohnungsfrage hinaus. Wenn wir über das Wohnungswesen sprechen, denken wir auch an das Wohnumfeld und das soziale Geflecht, zu dem auch Kleinbetriebe, politische Bedingungen et cetera gehören. Trotzdem haben wir vermutlich keine angemessene architektonische Lösung für die hier gestellte Frage gefunden, denn die Frage des sozialen Wohnungsbaus ist in erster Linie eine politische.

---

* The name refers to the Turkish word **Gecekondu** which means "built overnight" and is a reference to houses built by migrants moving from rural areas to the outskirts of small and large cities in Turkey. If built between dusk and dawn, the government was not allowed to tear down these houses without engaging in legal proceedings in court.

* Der Name geht zurück auf den türkischen Begriff **Gecekondu**, der „über Nacht errichtet" bedeutet und als Bezeichnung für die Häuser von Zuwanderern aus ländlichen Gebieten dient, die sich am Rand kleiner und großer türkischer Städte ansiedeln. Wurden diese Häuser zwischen Sonnenuntergang und Sonnenaufgang errichtet, durften sie von der Regierung nicht ohne gerichtlichen Beschluss abgerissen werden.

vivienda no es exclusiva de Berlín. En todas partes hace falta lo mismo, sobre todo cuando se trata de generar una nueva manera de pensar acerca de la vivienda pública. La vivienda pública hoy en día es insostenible si no está ligada a una infraestructura de apoyo que tenga sistemas sociales y económicos dentro de ella.

Sandy   *Wohnungsfrage* puso a Kotti & Co en la posición de comisionar a un arquitecto. El resultado no ha sido ni arquitectónico ni espacial, en el sentido de un nuevo diseño para la vivienda social del futuro. En cambio, *Wohnungsfrage* tomó en cuenta que nosotros operamos dentro de un contexto muy específico. El resultado no es una unidad de vivienda, sino una herramienta flexible y modular para permitir, en primer lugar, que los vecinos empiecen a comunicarse. Esta propuesta se extiende a la cuestión de la vivienda. Cuando hablamos de vivienda, también pensamos en los vecinos y en el tejido social, lo que incluye las economías, las condiciones políticas, etc. Sin embargo, probablemente no hemos encontrado una solución propiamente arquitectónica a la pregunta que se plantea aquí.

gerekliliği sadece Berlin'e özgü bir durum değil; aynı şeye her yerde ihtiyaç var, öncelikle de sosyal konut meselesi üzerine yeniden düşünürken. Bugün, sosyal ve ekonomik sistemler içeren bir altyapısal destek olmaksızın sosyal konutlandırmanın sürdürülebilmesi mümkün değildir.

Sandy   *Wohnungsfrage*, Kotti & Co'yu bir mimar görevlendirme pozisyonuna getirdi. Ortaya çıkan sonuç, geleceğin sosyal konutlarının tasarlanması bağlamında, ne mimari ne de mekânsaldı. Bunun yerine, çok özgün bir ortamda çalıştığımız göz önüne alınmalı. Sonuç, bir konut birimi değil ama öncelikle mahallelerin iletişim kurmaya başlayabileceği esnek, modüler bir araç oldu. Böylesi bir önerme konutlandırma konusunu genişletiyor. Konut sorunundan söz ederken ekonomi, politik koşullar ve benzerlerini içeren mahalleleri ve sosyal yapıyı da düşünüyoruz. Ancak, burada ortaya konulan soruna bulduğumuz çözüm tam anlamıyla bir mimari çözüm olmayabilir zira sosyal konut sorunu için çözüm öncelikle politiktir.

* El nombre viene de la palabra turca **Gecekondu**, que significa *"construido de la noche a la mañana"* y hace referencia a las casas construidas por los migrantes que se mueven de las zonas rurales a las afueras de las ciudades pequeñas y grandes en Turquía. Si se construían entre el anochecer y el amanecer, el gobierno no podía derribar estas casas sin enfrentar procesos judiciales en los tribunales.

* Türkçeden alınan Gecekondu terimi *"gece inşa edilmiş"* anlamını taşır ve Türkiye'de kırsal kesimlerden küçük veya büyük şehirlerin eteklerine gelen göçmenlerin inşa ettikleri konutları ima eder. Akşam karanlığı ile şafak vakti arasında inşa edilen bu evler mahkeme kararı olmaksızın hükümet tarafından yıkılamıyordu.

Scenarios

Szenarien

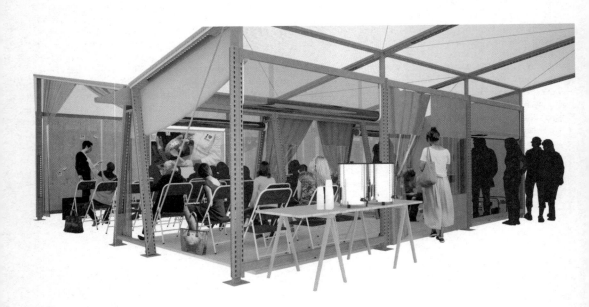

Public cinema
Collective viewing of informational movies and documentaries is an important element of neighborhood organization. An open-air cinema, protected by insulating curtains, activates the open spaces of the armature.

Öffentliches Kino
Info- und Dokumentarfilme gemeinsam anzuschauen ist ein wichtiger Teil der Nachbarschaftsarbeit. Das Retrofit Gecekondu kann durch Vorhänge verdunkelt und als Open-Air-Kino genutzt werden.

Cine Público
La proyección de películas y documentales informativos es un elemento importante de la organización social vecinal. Un cine al aire libre activa los espacios abiertos de la estructura, los cuales estan protegidos por una serie de cortinas aislantes.

Kamuya açık sinema
Bilgilendirici film ve belgesellerin beraber seyri komşuluk ilişkileri organizasyonunun önemli öğelerinden biridir. Retrofit gecekondu perdeler kullanılarak karartılır ve bir açık hava sineması olarak kullanılabilir.

Escenarios

Senaryolar

Market
The stand can be used for a local grocery market or street fair. The butterfly roof creates a symmetrical structure that opens outward, sheltering multiple vendors under a single neighborhood canopy.

Markt
Der Stand ist für lokale Lebensmittel- oder Straßenmärkte konzipiert. Das Schmetterlingsdach schafft eine symmetrische, nach außen offene Struktur – ein gemeinsames Dach, unter dem die Verkäufer ihre Produkte anbieten können.

Mercado
El quiosco se puede utilizar para un mercado local de comestibles o feria callejera. El techo mariposa crea una estructura simétrica que se abre hacia afuera, y sirve de cobijo a un buen número de vendedores bajo una sola cubierta vecinal.

Pazar yeri
Mimari birim yerel ürünler dükkanı ya da bir sokak panayırı için de kullanılabilir. Kelebek çatı simetrik yapısıyla dışarı doğru açılır ve bir dizi satıcıya bir komşuluk örtüsü altında barınma imkanı sağlar.

Assembly
The structure acts as an open forum for larger assemblies. The expandable armature increases its capacity from tenants' meetings, to a civic classroom, to a temporary urban parliament.

Versammlung
Das Metallgerüst dient als offenes Forum für größere Versammlungen. Es kann je nach Bedarf für Mietertreffen, Nachbarschaftsunterricht oder ein temporäres Stadtparlament erweitert werden.

Asamblea
La estructura actúa como un foro abierto para grandes asambleas, y su capacidad y escala se expanden incrementalmente, desde reuniones de arrendatarios, pasando por un aula cívica, hasta un parlamento urbano temporal.

Toplantı
Yapı büyük toplantılar için bir forum alanı işlevi görebiliyor. Genişletilebilir metal iskelet mekanın kiracı toplantılarından yurttaş sınıflarına ve hatta geçici şehir konseyi meclisine kadar çeşitli toplantılara ev sahipliği yapmasına imkan veriyor.

Protest stand
An information booth with display panels for posters and flyers. Here, the infrastructural system acts as a sociopolitical platform for the distribution of political knowledge and social organization.

Proteststand
Ein Informationsstand mit Auslagen für Plakate und Flugblätter, der als öffentliche Plattform für die Verbreitung von politischem Wissen und sozialer Organisation dient.

Quiosco de protesta
Un quiosco informativo con tableros para colgar carteles y volantes. Aquí el sistema infraestructural actúa como una plataforma sociopolítica para la distribución de organización social e información política.

Protesto mekanı
Afiş ve ilanlar için panolarla donatılmış bilgi kulübesi. Burada altyapı sistemi, sosyal organizasyon ve siyasi bilginin paylaşılması için sosyopolitik bir platform işlevi taşır.

Gallery
The pivoting panels create a didactic display system, serving as a framework of provocation that invites the audience to consider housing as a social and economic process.

Galerie
Die Drehtafeln erzeugen ein didaktisches Ausstellungssystem, das dem Publikum ermöglicht, Wohnen als sozialen und wirtschaftlichen Prozess zu erfahren.

Galería
Los paneles giratorios crean un sistema didáctico de exhibición, que actúa como un marco de provocación para invitar a la audiencia a considerar la vivienda como un proceso social y económico.

Galeri
Bir eksen etrafında dönen panolar eğitici bir sunum sistemi yaratarak izleyicileri, konutlandırmayı sosyal ve ekonomik bir süreç olarak sorunsallaştırmaya çağırırlar.

Workshop
The structure accommodates a series of partitions for pedagogical and practical activities, incubating local practices of craftsmanship to support cultural production and the local economy.

Werkstatt
Die Struktur kann in verschiedene Bereiche für pädagogische und handwerkliche Aktivitäten unterteilt werden. Die Förderung lokalen Handwerks stärkt kulturelle Produktion und Mikro-Ökonomien.

Taller
La estructura da cabida a una serie de particiones para actividades pedagógicas y de manufactura, incubando prácticas de artesanía local en apoyo a la producción cultural y a la economía.

Atölye
Atölye, farklı pedogojik aktiviteler ve el sanatları uygulamaları için bölümlere ayrılabilir. Yerel el sanatlarının desteklenmesi kültürel üretimi ve mikro ekonomiyi güçlendirir.

Shelter

The armature is a support system for informal urbanization, becoming an infrastructural framework on which to "stitch" and organize recycled waste from San Diego into Tijuana's slums.

Unterkunft

Das Metallgerüst dient als infrastrukturelle Unterstützung für informelle Urbanisierung. Die Rahmenkonstruktion bietet eine statische Basis, um recycelte Abfälle aus San Diego als Baumaterialien für den Wohnungsbau in den Slums von Tijuana wiederzuverwenden.

Abrigo
El armazón es un sistema de soporte para una urbanización informal, convirtiéndose en un marco infraestructural para organizar y adaptar los desechos de San Diego que se reciclan para los barrios bajos de Tijuana.

Barınma
Metal iskelet informel kentselleşme için bir destek sistemidir, San Diego'da geri kazanılan atık malzemenin Tijuana varoşlarında tekrar kullanımı için statik bir platform işlevi taşır.

Participants in the conversation

Gesprächsteilnehmer

Fatma Cakmak is a construction engineer and *Quartiersrätin* (voluntary district councilor). A mother of two children, she lives near Berlin's Kotbusser Tor, where she co-ordinates neighborhood activities, offers social counseling, and takes on many of the associated tasks of organization.

Teddy Cruz is an architect and Professor of Public Culture and Urbanization in the Visual Arts Department at the University of California, San Diego (UCSD). He is known internationally for his urban research on the Tijuana–San Diego border, focusing on the relationship between bottom-up urbanization and housing. **Fonna Forman** is a Professor of Political Theory at UCSD, and founding Director of the Center on Global Justice. She is best known for her revisionist work on Adam Smith, recuperating the ethical, social, spatial, and public dimensions of the modern political economy. Together they are directors of the UCSD Cross-Border Initiative, and Estudio Teddy Cruz + Forman, a research-based political and architectural practice in San Diego. Their work emphasizes urban conflict and informality as sites of intervention for rethinking public policy and civic infrastructure. They are presently investigating "citizenship culture" in the San Diego–Tijuana border region.

Melanie Dyck is a political scientist with work experience in caregiving, assistance, social counseling, and team and organization development. She works with the tenants' initiatives GSW23, Kotti & Co, and *Mietenvolksentscheid* (referendum on rents).

Jesko Fezer, designer and author, is Professor for Experimental Design at the Hochschule für bildende Künste Hamburg. He carries out architectural projects in co-operation with ifau, is co-founder of the bookstore Pro qm, and is part of the exhibition design studio Kooperative für Darstellungspolitik.

Ulrike Hamann is a cultural and political scientist and did her doctorate in the field of Postcolonial Studies at the Goethe-Universität in Frankfurt. She works as a lecturer and research assistant. Since co-founding Kotti & Co, she has been in charge of organization,

Fatma Cakmak ist Bauingenieurin und Quartiersrätin. Die Mutter zweier Töchter wohnt am Kottbusser Tor und organisiert dort die Nachbarschaft, macht Sozialberatung und übernimmt viele der organisatorischen Aufgaben.

Teddy Cruz ist Architekt und Professor für Öffentliche Kultur und Stadtplanung im Visual Arts Department der University of California in San Diego. International bekannt wurde er mit seiner Stadtforschung entlang der Grenze Tijuana/San Diego. Hier setzt er den Schwerpunkt auf die Beziehung zwischen einer Urbanisierung von unten und der Wohnungsfrage. **Fonna Forman** ist Professorin für Politikwissenschaften an der University of California in San Diego sowie Gründerin und Direktorin des *Center on Global Justice*. Sie ist vor allem für ihre wegweisende Arbeit über Adam Smith bekannt, in der sie die ethischen, räumlichen, sozialen und öffentlichen Dimensionen der modernen politischen Ökonomie zusammendenkt. Gemeinsam leiten sie die UCSD Cross-Border Initiative sowie das forschungsbasierte Architekturbüro Estudio Teddy Cruz + Forman in San Diego. Ihr Forschungsschwerpunkt liegt auf urbanen Konflikten und informellen Strukturen als Orten möglicher Intervention, anhand derer öffentliche Politik und zivile Infrastrukturen neu überdacht werden können. Derzeit arbeiten sie an einer Untersuchung einer „Bürgerkultur" in der Grenzregion San Diego/Tijuana.

Melanie Dyck ist Politikwissenschaftlerin mit Arbeitserfahrungen in Pflege, Assistenz, Sozialberatung sowie Team- und Organisationsentwicklung. Sie ist Mitarbeiterin bei den Mieterinitiativen GSW23, Kotti & Co und Mietenvolksentscheid.

Jesko Fezer, Gestalter und Autor, ist Professor für Experimentelles Design an der Hochschule für bildende Künste Hamburg. In Kooperation mit ifau realisiert er Architekturprojekte. Er ist Mitbegründer der Buchhandlung Pro qm sowie Teil des Ausstellungsgestaltungsstudios Kooperative für Darstellungspolitik.

Ulrike Hamann ist Kultur- und Politikwissenschaftlerin und hat an der Goethe-Universität Frankfurt im

Participantes en la conversacion

Katılımcılar

Fatma Cakmak es ingeniera de la construcción y *Quartiersrätin* (concejal de distrito voluntaria). Madre de dos hijos, vive cerca del Kotbusser Tor en Berlín, donde coordina las actividades del barrio, da asesoría social y asume muchas de las tareas asociativas de la organización.

Teddy Cruz es arquitecto y profesor de Cultura pública y urbanización en el Departamento de artes visuales de la Universidad de California en San Diego (UCSD). Es reconocido internacionalmente por su investigación urbana sobre la frontera Tijuana-San Diego, centrada en la relación entre la urbanización informal y la vivienda. **Fonna Forman** es profesora de Teoría política en la UCSD, y directora y fundadora del Centro de Justicia Global. Es mejor conocida por su trabajo revisionista sobre Adam Smith, en el que recupera los aspectos éticos, sociales, espaciales y públicos de la economía política moderna. Juntos son directores de la Iniciativa Transfronteriza de la UCSD, y del Estudio Teddy Cruz + Forman, una práctica política y arquitectónica localizada en San Diego. Su trabajo enfatiza los conflictos urbanos y la informalidad como sitios de intervención para repensar las políticas públicas y la infraestructura cívica. Actualmente investigan la "cultura ciudadana" en la región fronteriza San Diego-Tijuana.

Melanie Dyck es una especialista en ciencias políticas con experiencia de trabajo en cuidados, asistencia, orientación social y desarrollo de organizaciones y equipos. Trabaja con las iniciativas de los inquilinos GSW23, Kotti & Co y *Mietenvolksentscheid* .

Jesko Fezer, diseñador y autor, es profesor de Diseño experimental en la Hochschule für bildende Künste en Hamburgo. Lleva a cabo proyectos arquitectónicos en cooperación con ifau, es cofundador de la librería Pro qm, y es parte del estudio de diseño de exposiciones Kooperative für Darstellungspolitik.

Ulrike Hamann es una científica cultural y política y realizó su doctorado en el campo de los Estudios postcoloniales en la Goethe-Universität de Frankfurt. Trabaja como profesora y asistente de investigación.

Fatma Cakmak inşaat mühendisi ve mahalle konseyi üyesi. İki çocuk annesi olan Çakmak Kottbusser Tor'da oturuyor ve bu mahallede komşu inisiyatiflerini düzenliyor, sosyal danışmanlık yapıyor, organizasyonla ilgili görevler üstleniyor.

Teddy Cruz mimar ve San Diego'daki Kalifornia Üniversitesi'nin görsel sanatlar bölümünde kamusal kültür ve kentselleşme profesörü. Tijuana/San Diego sınırındaki şehirleşme alanında yaptığı ve aşağıdan yukarı kentselleşmeyle konutlandırmanın arasındaki ilişkiye odaklanan araştırmayla uluslarası arenada tanınıyor. **Fonna Forman** San Diedo'daki Kaliforniya Üniversitesi'nde siyasi kuram profesörü ve *Center on Global Justice*'nin (Küresel Adalet Merkezi) kurucu başkanı. Adam Smith'i yeniden ele alan ve bu bağlamda modern siyasi iktisadın ahlaki, toplumsal, mekânsal ve kamusal boyutlarını toparlayan çalışmalarıyla tanınıyor. Beraberce UCSD Cross-Border Initiative (Kaliforniya Üniversitesi, San Diego, Sınır Ötesi Girişimi) ve San Diego›da araştırma bazlı siyasi ve mimari çalışmalar yapan Estudio Teddy Cruz + Forman'ı yönetiyorlar. Çalışmalarında kentsel çatışmalar ve informelliğe, kamusal politikaların ve kentsel altyapının tekrar ele alınıp yeniden düşünülmesinin mevzileri olarak odaklanıyorlar. Şu anda San Diego-Tijuana sınır bölgesinde ‹yurttaşlık kültürü› konusunu araştırıyorlar.

Melanie Dyck, siyaset bilimci; bakım, destek, sosyal danışmanlık, ekip ve organizasyon geliştirme alanlarında iş tecrübesi var. GSW23, Kotti & Co ve *Mietenvolksentscheid* isimli kiracı girişimlerinde aktif.

Jesko Fezer, tasarımcı ve yazar, Hamburg Güzel Sanatlar Akademisi'nde deneysel tasarım profesörü. ifau ile işbirliği yaparak mimari projelere hayat veriyor, Pro qm isimli kitap dükkanının kurucularından ve keza Kooperative für Darstellungspolitik (Sunum Politikaları İmecesi) isimli sergileme tasarımı stüdyosunun unsurlarından.

Ulrike Hamann kültür ve siyaset bilimleri okudu ve ardından Frankfurt Goethe-Üniversitesi'nde Postcolonial Studies (Sömürgecilik sonrası dönem

co-ordination, public relations, and political and academic analyses. She lives at Berlin's Kottbusser Tor.

Alexander Sandy Kaltenborn is co-founder of the tenants' collective Kotti & Co. In his other life, he is a communications designer, and since 1999 has run the agency image-shift.net | visual communication & other misunderstandings.

Angelika Levi studied at the Deutsche Film- und Fernsehakademie Berlin (German Film and Television Academy Berlin—DFFB). Her works have been shown at international film and video festivals since 1985, winning several awards. Alongside her own projects, she works as a screenplay writer, editor, and lecturer. Her works are distributed by Arsenal—Institut für Film und Videokunst. Angelika Levi lives and works in Berlin.

Zehra Ulutürk is assistant to a medical doctor and *Quartiersrätin* (voluntary district councilor). A mother of four children, she lives at Berlin's Kottbusser Tor and actively helped shape Kotti & Co with her analyses and passion for debate.

Bereich der Postcolonial Studies promoviert. Sie arbeitet als Lehrbeauftragte und wissenschaftliche Mitarbeiterin. Seit sie Kotti & Co mitgegründet hat, ist sie für Organisation, Koordination, Öffentlichkeitsarbeit, politische und wissenschaftliche Analysen zuständig. Sie wohnt am Kottbusser Tor.

Alexander Sandy Kaltenborn ist Mitbegründer der Mietergemeinschaft Kotti & Co. In seinem anderen Leben ist er Kommunikationsdesigner und betreibt seit 1999 das Büro image-shift.net / visuelle Kommunikation und andere Missverständnisse.

Angelika Levi studierte an der Deutschen Film- und Fernsehakademie Berlin. Seit 1985 werden ihre Arbeiten auf internationalen Film- und Videofestivals gezeigt und ausgezeichnet. Neben eigenen Projekten ist sie als Drehbuchautorin, Cutterin und Dozentin beschäftigt. Ihre Arbeiten befinden sich im Verleih „Arsenal — Institut für Film und Videokunst". Angelika Levi wohnt und arbeitet in Berlin.

Zehra Ulutürk ist Arzthelferin und Quartiersrätin. Die Mutter von vier Kindern wohnt am Kottbusser Tor und hat Kotti & Co von Anfang an aktiv durch ihre Analysen und Diskussionsfreudigkeit mitgestaltet.

Desde que fue cofundadora de Kotti & Co, ha estado a cargo de la organización, coordinación, relaciones públicas y del análisis político y académico. Vive cerca del Kottbusser Tor en Berlín.

Alexander Sandy Kaltenborn es cofundador del colectivo de inquilinos Kotti & Co. En su otra vida, es un diseñador de comunicaciones, y desde 1999 ha dirigido la agencia image-shift.net / visuelle Kommunikation und andere Missverständnisse.

Angelika Levi estudió en la Deutsche Film- und Fernsehakademie de Berlín (la Academia de Cine y Televisión alemana en Berlin – DFFB). Sus obras se han exhibido en festivales internacionales de cine y vídeo desde 1985, y han ganado varios premios. Además de sus propios proyectos, trabaja como guionista, editora y profesora. Sus obras son distribuidas por Arsenal – Institut für Film und Videokunst. Angelika Levi vive y trabaja en Berlín.

Zehra Ulutürk es ayudante médica y *Quartiersrätin* (concejal de distrito voluntaria). Madre de cuatro hijos, vive cerca del Kotbusser Tor en Berlín y ha contribuido activamente a conformar Kotti & Co con su análisis y su pasión por el debate.

araştırmaları) dalında doktora yaptı. Öğretim ve araştırma görevlisi olarak çalışıyor. Kotti & Co'nın kurucularından biri olarak organizasyon, eşgüdüm, halkla ilişkiler, siyasi ve bilimsel analizlerden sorumlu. Yaşamını Kottbusser Tor'da sürdürüyor.

Alexander Sandy Kaltenborn, kiracı girişimi Kotti & Co'nun kurucularından biri. Diğer hayatındaysa iletişim tasarımcısı ve 1999 yılından beri image-shift.net / visuelle Kommunikation und andere Missverständnisse isimli tasarım bürosunu yönetiyor.

Angelika Levi Berlin'deki Almanya Film- ve Televizyon Akademisi'nde okudu. 1985'den beri bir çok eseri uluslararası film ve video festivallerinde gösterildi, ödüller kazandı. Kendi projeleri dışında senaryo yazarı, kurgucu ve öğretim görevlisi olarak çalışmalarını sürdürüyor. Yapıtlarına ulaşmak Arsenal – Institut für Film und Videokunst üzerinden mümkün. Angelika Levi Berlin'de ikâmet ediyor ve çalışıyor.

Zehra Ulutürk doktor yardımcısı ve mahalle konseyi üyesi. Dört çocuğu olan Ulutürk Kottbusser Tor'da oturuyor. Kotti & Co'nun şekillenmesine kuruluş günlerinden itibaren analizleri ve tartışmacı kişiliğiyle aktif katkıda bulundu.

Sandy   Many of the immigrant economies here are family-run. They are a mix of formal and informal organization of labor without distinction between the private and the public sphere. This perspective also reflects on our understanding of the economy, which reaches beyond that considered in the classical sense "work."

Gecekondu, Bethaniendamm, Berlin

Ulrike   Coming to some conclusions from our discussions about the 1:1 model, I think we need an architectural structure that is both flexible in its usage and that can also migrate to other neighborhoods for their meetings and protests. However, it should not only be working as a hub for political protest and information, but also as a social space, a protective space, as shelter, and for the economic dimension of housing and protest—for selling food or home-made products.

Teddy   We are excited about the idea of a light, flexible "station" that can occupy a particular empty space in the neighborhood, and support new small-scale economic activity that emerges from the everyday practices and social relations among tenants. This could potentially connect the lack of housing affordability to issues of unemployment. This does not undercut the argument for which Kotti & Co have been fighting—that rents must be lowered and secure—but in addition to this premise, one that requires state, top-down accountability, we argue that housing must enable bottom-up sensibilities and capacities for economic creativity that benefits tenants. The urgent need to make this connection between spaces of local productivity and housing units is not unique to Berlin; the same is required everywhere, primarily in the rethinking of public housing. Public housing today is unsustainable without an infrastructure of support that has social and economic systems threaded within it.

die architektonische Struktur auch eine Art Unterkunft bieten können.

Jesko   Genau. Beim Wohnen geht es allerdings nicht allein um Schutz. Auch die Orte rund um den Wohnraum müssen reklamiert werden, sie können zu lokalen Produktionsräumen oder auch Begegnungszentren werden: Räume, die Mietern die Möglichkeit zu praktischen Verbesserungen ihres eigenen Lebens geben und ihnen ein Mitspracherecht bei der Planung von Wohnraum und Änderungen des Status quo gewähren.

Teddy   Wirtschaftliche Probleme lassen sich eventuell auch dadurch angehen, dass man den Treffpunkt, den wir errichten wollen, zu einem wirtschaftlichen Inkubator macht und so unterstreicht, dass das Problem bezahlbarer Mieten auch mit dem Thema Arbeitsplätze zu tun hat. Ich stelle mir das so vor, dass sich in vielen Wohnungen kleine Betriebe entwickeln, dass die Menschen hier selbst etwas produzieren. Der Treffpunkt könnte sie unterstützen und eine Verbindung zwischen dieser Art von Produktion im privaten Raum und der Straße herstellen.

Sandy   Viele der migrantischen Betriebe hier sind in Familienhand. Es handelt sich um eine Mischung aus formell und informell organisierter Arbeit, bei der zwischen privatem und öffentlichem Bereich wenig unterschieden wird. Diese Perspektive entspricht auch unserem Begriff von Ökonomie, der über das klassische Verständnis von „Arbeit" hinausgeht.

Ulrike   Letztendlich haben unsere Diskussionen über das 1:1-Modell ergeben, dass wir eine Architektur benötigen, die eine flexible Nutzung ermöglicht und sich in andere Viertel übertragen lässt, um auch dort für Treffen und Proteste genutzt zu werden. Sie sollte jedoch nicht nur als politisches Protest- und Informationszentrum dienen, sondern auch als sozialer Raum und Schutzraum, als Zuflucht, sowie für die wirtschaftliche Dimension der Wohnungsfrage – für den selbstorganisierten Verkauf von Lebensmitteln oder selbstgemachten Produkten.

Teddy   Wir finden die Idee einer leichten, flexiblen „Station" sehr spannend, die einen bisher ungenutzten Platz im Viertel besetzen und neue wirtschaftliche Aktivitäten im kleinen Rahmen unterstützen kann, die sich wiederum aus der alltäglichen Praxis und den sozialen Beziehungen zwischen den Mietern ergeben. Dadurch ließe sich möglicherweise das Problem fehlenden bezahlbaren Wohnraums mit Themen rund um die Arbeitslosigkeit verbinden. Die eigentliche Sache, für die Kotti & Co kämpft – dass die Mieten gesenkt werden und sicher sein müssen – wird damit ja nicht unterlaufen. Wir betonen nur, dass zusätzlich zur

The series *Wohnungsfrage* is edited by /
Die Reihe *Wohnungsfrage* wird herausgegeben von /
La serie *Wohnungsfrage* ha sido editada por /
Wohnungsfrage dizisini yayına hazırlayanlar
Jesko Fezer, Christian Hiller, Nikolaus Hirsch,
Wilfried Kuehn, Hila Peleg.

Editing / Redaktion / Redacción / Redaksiyon:
Jesko Fezer, Martin Hager, Christian Hiller,
Alexandra Nehmer

Editorial assistance / Redaktionsassistenz /
Asistencia editorial / Redaksiyon yardımcısı:
Franziska Janetzky

Translations / Übersetzungen /
Traducciones / Tercümeler

to German / ins Deutsche / al alemán / Almanca'ya:
Gaby Gehlen, Anja Schulte

to Spanish / ins Spanische / al español / İspanyolca'ya:
Rafael Segovia, Katerina Valdivia Bruch

to English / ins Englische / al inglés / İngilizce'ye:
Tim Jones

to Turkish / ins Türkische / al turco / Türkçe'ye:
Ali Selman, Monika & Hulki Demirel

Copy-editing / Lektorat / Revisión de texto / Editörlük

German / Deutsch / Alemán / Almanca:
Claudius Prößer

English / Englisch / Inglés / İngilizce: Mandi Gomez

Turkish / Türkisch / Turco / Türkçe: Hulki Demirel

Graphic design / Grafische Gestaltung /
Diseño gráfico / Grafik tasarım:
Studio Matthias Görlich

Lithography / Lithografie / Litografía / Litografi:
Felix Scheu

Typefaces / Schrift / Tipografía / Harf karakteri:
Eesti Display, Sectra (Grilli Type)

Printing / Druck / Impresión / Baskı:
PögeDruck, Leipzig

Binding / Bindung / Encuadernación / Cilt:
Buchbinderei Mönch, Leipzig

Published by / Erschienen bei / Publicado por /
Yayınlayan:
Spector Books
Harkortstraße 10, D-04107 Leipzig
www.spectorbooks.com

Distribution / Vertrieb / Distribución / Dağıtım:
Germany, Austria: GVA, Gemeinsame Verlags-
auslieferung Göttingen GmbH & Co. KG,
www.gva-verlage.de
Switzerland: AVA Verlagsauslieferung AG, www.ava.ch
France, Belgium: Interart Paris, www.interart.fr
UK: Central Books Ltd, www.centralbooks.com
USA, Canada: RAM Publications+Distribution Inc.,
www.rampub.com
Australia, New Zealand: Perimeter Distribution,
www.perimeterdistribution.com

Kotti & Co, Project team / Projektteam /
Equipo del proyecto / Proje ekibi

Project management / Projektmanagement /
Gestión de proyecto / Proje yönetimi:
Fatma Cakmak, Ulrike Hamann,
Alexander Sandy Kaltenborn, Angelika Levi

Cooperation / Mitarbeit / Cooperación / Katılanlar:
Aynur Adigüzel, Melanie Dyck, Tashy Endres,
Richard Fährmann, Jale Öztekin, Tahir Sözen,
Tuncay Tükrükcü, Ahmed Tuncer, Neriman Tuncer,
Zehra Ulutürk, Sabryie Yildiz

Estudio Teddy Cruz + Forman, Project team /
Projektteam / Equipo del proyecto / Proje ekibi

Directors / Leiter / Directores / Yöneticiler:
Teddy Cruz + Fonna Forman

Project Manager / Projektmanager /
Gestión del proyecto / Proje müdürü:
Brendan Finney

Structural engineer partner / Statik-Partner /
Socio ingeniero estructural / Statik mühendisi:
Alejandro Barajas

Assistants / Assistenten / Asistentes / Asistanlar:
Irene Garguilo, Nada Maani, Blake Thomas

Mecalux Project manager / Projektmanager Mecalux /
Gestor del proyecto Mecalux / Mecalux proje müdürü:
David Felix Mancera

Mecalux CEO / Geschäftsführung Mecalux /
Director general Mecalux / Mecalux CEO:
Angel de Arriba Serrano

Wohnungsfrage Team:

Concept and program / Konzept und Programm /
Concepto y programación / Konsept ve program:
Jesko Fezer, Nikolaus Hirsch, Wilfried Kuehn,
Hila Peleg

Project leader / Projektleitung /
Director del proyecto / Proje lideri:
Annette Bhagwati, Zdravka Bajovic

Research and Publications / Forschung und
Publikationen / Investigación y publicaciones /
Araştırma ve yayınlar: Christian Hiller

Research and project coordination Exhibition /
Forschung und Projektkoordination Ausstellung /
Investigación y coordinación de proyecto Exposición /
Araştırma ve proje eşgüdümü – Sergi:
Zdravka Bajovic

Project coordination Exhibition / Projektkoordination
Ausstellung / Coordinación de proyecto Exposición /
Proje eşgüdümü – Sergi: Jessica Páez

Project coordination Academy / Projektkoordination
Akademie / Coordinación de proyecto Academia /
Proje eşgüdümü – Akademi: Stefan Aue

Assistant to the project leader / Assistenz der
Projektleitung / Asistente del director de proyecto /
Proje lideri yardımcısı: Dunja Sallan

Project assistance / Projektassistenz / Asistencia
al proyecto / Proje asistanı: Franziska Janetzky,
Ben Mohai, Alexandra Nehmer

Production management / Produktionsleitung /
Dirección de producción / Yapım yönetimi:
Thomas Burkhard

Intern / Praktikantin / Practicante / Stajyer:
Deborah Avanzato

Wohnungsfrage takes place as part of the HKW project
100 Years of Now (2015–2018). / *Wohnungsfrage* findet
im Rahmen des HKW-Projekts *100 Jahre Gegenwart*
(2015–2018) statt. / *Wohnungsfrage* se realiza en el
marco del proyecto de la HKW *100 Years of Now*
(2015–2018). / *Wohnungsfrage* HKW'nin *100 Jahre
Gegenwart* (2015–2018) isimli projesinin çerçevesinde
gerçekleşmektedir.
www.hkw.de/now

The Haus der Kulturen der Welt is a division of /
Das Haus der Kulturen der Welt ist ein Geschäfts-
bereich der / La Haus der Kulturen der Welt es
una división de / Haus der Kulturen der Welt bu
kurumun bir parçasıdır
Kulturveranstaltungen des Bundes in Berlin GmbH
(KBB).

Director / Intendant / Director / Yönetmen:
Bernd Scherer

General manager / Kaufmännische Geschäfts-
führerin / Gerente general / Genel müdür:
Charlotte Sieben

Chair of the Advisory Board / Vorsitzende des
Aufsichtsrats / Presidenta de la junta de asesores /
Danışma kurulu başkanı: Staatsministerin Prof.
Monika Grütters MdB

The Haus der Kulturen der Welt is funded by /
Das Haus der Kulturen der Welt wird gefördert durch /
La Haus der Kulturen der Welt recibe el apoyo
financiero de / Haus der Kulturen der Welt bu
kurmlardan destek almaktadır:

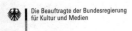

Printed in Germany
First edition
This volume is part of a two-piece edition.
It is published jointly with:
Kotti & Co, *und deswegen sind wir hier.*
ISBN 978-3-95905-050-0